"A sparkling debut, *Womankind* proves to me that sisterhood is possible among women who have little more in common than being women. With the compassionate and lyrical voice of a nurse who has spent years volunteering for medical projects from Belize to Kosovo, Nancy Harless surprises and rewards us with her lively accounts of girls and women who manage to flourish in the midst of poverty, war, and the challenges of living in a man's world. If you've ever wondered if there really is a unique spiritual connection among women, *Womankind* offers poetic proof in story after story about women who help each other to live rich and abundant lives, who honour nature and spirit, and who move through the rigors of their daily lives with courage, resilience, and hope. Equally enlightening is Harless's insightful introspection about her complicated role as a First World volunteer in countries whose futures are risky at best, and her continuous struggle to reach across the boundaries of nationality and language in the loving gestures of sisterhood. As an orange seller in Belize says to Harless one day: "Life can stretch your soul or tear your spirit." Thanks to Harless's inspiring pen, the women of *Womankind* will make your soul and spirit soar. An eye-opening and inspiring read."

Susan Sanchez-Causal, co-author of *Chicken Soup for the Latino Soul*

"Nancy Leigh Harless is fresh new writer who braids narrative threads of true stories about ordinary women from all over the world, living in extraordinary circumstances. These stories show us not only who these women are, but who we are and the universality of our lives and lessons. This remarkable collection of legacies will make readers cry, and laugh, and celebrate the community of women worldwide."

LeAnn Thieman, co-author of *Chicken Soup for the Nurse's Soul*

"Nurse practitioner Nancy Harless has written a moving collection of short stories based on her intimate encounters with strong, courageous women around the globe. A skilled, sensitive storyteller, her tales in Womankind transcend cultural, racial, and gender boundaries to touch the human heart."

Marie Delgado Travis, award-winning Latino
writer and author of La Ventana/The Window

"If you've ever wondered what the expression 'heart of a woman' means, read this book and you will understand exactly what makes a woman's heart tick. Through these powerful stories of fascinating women and girls from around the globe, Nancy Harless reveals and celebrates the integrity, ingenuity, strength, and sheer beauty of the feminine spirit."

Colleen Sell, editor of the bestselling *A Cup of Comfort*
anthology series and co-author of 10-*Minute Zen*

"*Womankind,* by Nancy Leigh Harless, is a deftly woven glimpse into the women of other cultures—how they live, work, and cope in very difficult situations such as poverty and war. This sensitive, insightful collection showcases the author's ability to connect to others and her surroundings through understanding and compassion, as well as food and humor, and does so without being judgmental."

Susan Brady, editor of *The World Is a Kitchen*

WOMANKIND

Connection & Wisdom Around the World

To Mary Jane,

Enjoy the journey!

Amy Leigh Haless

NANCY LEIGH HARLESS

WOMANKIND

Connection & Wisdom Around the World

TATE PUBLISHING & *Enterprises*

Published by Tate Publishing & Enterprises, LLC
127 E. Trade Center Terrace | Mustang, Oklahoma 73064 USA
1.888.361.9473 | www.tatepublishing.com

Tate Publishing is committed to excellence in the publishing industry. The company reflects the philosophy established by the founders, based on Psalms 68:11,
"The Lord gave the word and great was the company of those who published it."

Book design copyright © 2007 by Tate Publishing, LLC. All rights reserved.
Cover design by Elizabeth A. Mason
Interior design by Steven Jeffrey

Published in the United States of America

ISBN: 978-1-60247-567-0
1. Non-fiction: Short Stories: Inspirational
07.08.27

DEDICATION

For Barbara Ann

ACKNOWLEDGMENTS

I wish to thank Joan Drury for the remarkable gift of a writing residency for women, where my memories of amazing, strong, and beautiful women were first lifted from the secret pages of my journals and began to shape shift into the stories of Womankind. Words fall short of describing my gratitude for that incredible writing time and space called Norcroft. And to all my fellow writers, "The Norcrofties," I thank you for your consistent support.

To Deb Engle, my friend, mentor, and inspiration, thank you for all that you are. When our paths crossed synchronistically years ago, careening around steep turns and switchbacks of the narrow Guatemala highland roads, I was given a blessing—the gift of your friendship. I was then, and am today, blessed.

I thank Ed, friend and mentor, for lending a man's perspective on all the women's stories.

To the Daybreak Women of Saint Johns United Church of Christ, Fort Madison, Iowa—those who have gone on before, as well as those who walk with me today—thank you for challenging and encouraging me. The narratives of *Womankind* might not have been told without your willing ears as story catchers.

Thank you to the prose arm of the Society of Great River Poets of Burlington, Iowa, for all your delightful and thoughtful feedback. A special thanks to Corrine and Ron Kahl, proofreaders extraordinaire!

I applaud the Writing Group of the University Women of Iowa City, Iowa, for your "ruthlessly kind" and always right-on critiques. Thank you for your support and positive responses.

To my daughters and stepdaughters—all amazing women in your own right—for your patient readings and comments, and especially to Mary, for the final proofreading, a huge thank you!

And to my rock, Norm, who has taken me around the world and brought me back home again. Thank you for always believing in me and, more importantly, believing in us.

TABLE OF CONTENTS

Foreword 13
Introduction 17

Section One - Dance Into a Bright New Day 23
       Joy in the Morning 25
       Maria Gabriel 31
       The Peaches 35
       Dance, Baby Girl, Dance 43

Section Two - All in Her Day's Work 59
       A Picnic in Hoghoost 61
       Making the Small Tortilla 71
       The World is a Dangerous Place 79
       In God's Palm 85

Section Three - Wherever There is Great Love 91
       Over Coffee with Sister Filje 93
       Lillian's Life 99
       Please Help My Son Not Die 107

Section Four - Many Truths, Many Ways 115
       Socorro's Secret 117
       I am a Curandera 129
       Rainbow of Gladiolas 135

Section Five - In the Shadows 141
       A Somber Decision 143
       Norma Jane 151
       Amid the Children and Chicken 157

Section Six - Earned Wisdom 163
       You Are the Nurse? 165
       A Mermaid's Bounty 173
       Only a Nurse 177
       Choices 185

Appendices 191

FOREWORD

*F*or Nancy Harless, travel, writing, and healing represent a sacred trinity. She didn't know this just ten years ago when she embarked on her first trip outside the US—a month-long cultural exchange to Guatemala and Belize. At the time, she was working for Planned Parenthood as a nurse practitioner. She'd had years of experience in healing, but travel and writing were as foreign to her as Guatemala's Mayan ruins.

I was fortunate to share that Central American trip with Nancy. We started our journey in Chicago, where we practiced Spanish verb tenses at a Berlitz school during the day and consumed deep-dish pizza in the evening. I immediately liked her for her sense of humor, her persistence in learning how to say, "My husband and I have eight children," in Spanish, and her refreshing sense of wonder and compassion.

Through the next few weeks, as we journeyed to every part of Guatemala and the adjoining country of Belize, I observed something important happening to Nancy. Her voice became stronger, her message more clear. By the time we neared the end of our trip, she was standing up in front of Guatemalan leaders proclaiming who she was in Spanish. "Mi esposo y yo tenemos ocho niños," she would say, immediately winning over her audience with this description of her large family. Even though she couldn't converse fluently, she created instant and lasting connections through her smile and genuine interest.

I noticed this happening everywhere we went. We toured a floating dental clinic on the Rio Dulce River, where an American man had built a boarding school for Mayan children in the jungles of northern Guatemala. We toured hospitals in Guatemala City, where indigent people waited in dirty hallways for a bed and basic medication. And we visited a school in the remote mountain village of Pachilá, where children ran barefoot and helped their mothers and grandmothers cook over three-stone hearths.

Along the way, Nancy was paying attention. She observed the smiles of young girls who clung to their mother's skirts, noticed the shy abandon of women as they slipped away from the watchful eyes of their husbands, and saw the fatigue on the faces of young women who had borne four or five children by the time they were twenty. The details of these women's lives became a part of her.

I suppose practically everyone who goes on a cultural exchange has grand plans to hold onto the experience once they come home. They resolve to stay in touch with their home hosts, send money back to the developing country, and return again someday. Most people never do. But Nancy did.

A few months after that trip, Nancy and her husband, Norm, returned to Belize, where they built a women's clinic that offered medical check-ups and birth control. Nancy put out the word, and before long women from the surrounding villages walked or rode the bus to the clinic, seeking out Nancy for honest advice, wisdom, and compassion. Nancy instinctively knew that her role was not to prescribe changes in these women's lives, but to offer them options they'd never experienced before. In gratitude, they invited her to their homes, told her their most intimate stories, and came to her clinic from miles away to learn how to "have no more babies."

For Nancy, this was simply the beginning. She found additional nurses to staff the clinic, freeing her to turn her attention to other needs around the world. She volunteered to serve on a medical team in Kosovo and traveled to Peru to learn the healing arts of the Incas. At this writing, she and Norm are about to leave for China, where she will no doubt find others in need and new ways to help them.

Nancy is that rare person who, through sheer persistence and a blend of practical and visionary ideas, continues to see the good that can be done in this world. Through her travels, she's discovered that much of that good comes from telling stories. In fact, for women who have experienced the horrors of war, the oppression of religious intolerance, and a poverty of choices in everything from the clothes they're allowed to wear to the children they're expected to bear, sharing personal stories is one of the best ways to heal.

That's what *Womankind* represents: a collective healing, not just for the women Nancy writes about, but for everyone who reads these insightful glimpses into the universal concerns women face. This is a book that incites thought, examination, and change. It is a celebration of women, and a measure of how far we need to go to achieve a greater sense of our selves.

Nancy achieved that sense of self-empowerment through travel, caring for others, and giving voice to those who were silent. My hope is that she will rub off on you as she has on me, inspiring us all to take that first step into the unknown and to make it a better place before we return, forever changed, back home.

- Debra Landwehr Engle, author of *Grace From the Garden:*
Changing the World One Garden at a Time

INTRODUCTION

$\mathcal{B}$lack tattered ribbons fluttered from trees and fences. A dark-skinned young man wearing army fatigues, machine gun slung casually over one shoulder, stood at the entrance of the gated community. He motioned for us to stop. Our passports were passed forward, photos scrutinized, handed back, and with an abrupt "Gracias," we were motioned forward.

It was 1997. I had been chosen to be part of a professional exchange program to Guatemala and Belize sponsored by The Rotary International. We arrived in Guatemala City only three months after the peace treaty was signed, ending a more than thirty-year Civil War. The peace accord called for incorporation of the guerilla rebel forces into the mainstream. Demobilizations such as this are often accompanied by sharp increases in crime. Guatemala was no exception.

Krista, one of the young women in my host family, shared her deepest fear with me. "Nearly every family has someone kidnapped," she said. "Sometimes they take old women, but usually just the young ones—like me. The black ribbons are for the women—one for every woman who has been taken. They are requests for prayers for their safe return."

It was a life-changing month of contrasts spent exploring other cultures from the inside. I waltzed at the Ambassador's Ball among men wearing Armani suits and women dressed in sequins and satin then visited a remote mountain village where barefoot women ground corn by hand as they prepared the daily meal of tortillas. I attended a wedding more lavish than anything I could imagine and visited a hospital where trash lined the hallways and the women crowded together two-to-a-bed after they delivered their babies. I played ring-around-the-rosy with dark-eyed little girls dressed in colorful hand-embroidered *huipiles*, just like their grandmothers had worn.

I felt as though I'd been plucked from my safe American home, tumbled about in a whirlwind for a month, then set back down in the same small Midwestern spot. But nothing would ever be the same again.

Most of my previous travel involved white-sand beaches. Now that sort of journey no longer held appeal. A fire and a fury had been unleashed inside me. I wanted to explore—to see inside other cultures, understand their people, and make every place I visited better in some small way. Inspired, I took a hiatus from my job as a nurse practitioner to do volunteer work.

An English-only speaker, it seemed a logical fit for me to team up with an agency working to improve the health of women in Belize, where English is the official language. Rotarian Doctor Coye introduced me to Julia Castello, the Director of Nursing in Belize. Through the miracle of the Internet and a year of correspondence, a project took shape. It involved working with the Belize Family Life Association (BFLA) to reopen a long-closed Women's Clinic in the southernmost part of the country.

On market day the buses came from distant villages. The tiny Mayan women wearing a bright rainbow of traditional dresses were already waiting when I arrived at the clinic every morning. Women of all ages, bent by time and circumstance, old prematurely from the weight of too many pregnancies, told me again and again, "I want to make no more babies." I was happy to be able to provide basic healthcare, including family planning, for these women.

The clinic remains open today. For several years it was staffed by volunteers; however, in 2005 BFLA was able to hire a Belizean nurse who runs the clinic today largely through the generosity of international donations.

While working in Belize during the spring of 1999, NATO forces dropped bombs on Kosovo on the other side of the world and brought an end to years of escalating ethnic cleansing. When I heard this over Radio Free America, the only station available in Punta Gorda, I knew that I needed to go to Kosovo next.

The following year I spent the millennium summer working in

the war recovery effort as part of a mission to implement modern healthcare in the Balkans. I came to know my Kosovar staff very well. Each was a remarkable woman who demonstrated caring, compassion, and a readiness to go that extra kilometer for their patients. Memories of these brave women rebuilding their lives and their country will stay with me forever. Each had a poignant story to share and the deep need to have their story heard. It was in Kosovo I came to understand the gift of being fully present.

I travel often now—always on a shoestring—usually off the well-traveled road. Each journey seems to lead me to the next. An interest in alternative healing sparked in Guatemala led me to the highlands of Peru. Fascination with indigenous midwifery practices that began in Peru drew me repeatedly to Mexico, particularly to the CASA project of San Miguel de Allende, where young women are brought to the city, given three years of modern training, and then sent back to bring twentieth century healthcare to their remote villages. Meeting up with old friends in Mexico gave rise to the sharing of a sailing adventure off the coast of Panama and blessed me with the lesson of living minimally.

To date, I have lived in or visited fifteen countries, and what I have come to know for sure is this: Although the colors of our skin may vary and our ways of being are many, women everywhere are more alike than different.

In every corner of the globe I have sensed the sisterhood. I have seen women struggle, sometimes against daunting odds. I have seen them nearly break under the weight of their lives. And I have felt an abundance of spirit, of wisdom, and of connection with these very women—ordinary women who live with extraordinary grace.

We have laughed together. We have cried. Through the sharing of her everyday story, each woman's life has been validated; my own profoundly enriched. For the honor of being an ear for so many women, so many stories, I am deeply grateful. Now through the telling, I hope to provide her voice.

Margaret Mead said, "It has been women's task throughout history to go on believing in life when there was almost no hope." I have witnessed this truth. However, the purpose of

Womankind is not to dwell on the many hardships women face. It is to celebrate their lives. My wish is that the hope, the joy, the wisdom, and the love that shines through each of these amazing, strong women will resonate deep in your bones and illumine your path.

SECTION ONE

DANCE INTO A BRIGHT NEW DAY

Joy in the Morning

"THOSE WHO DON'T KNOW HOW TO WEEP WITH THEIR
WHOLE HEART, DON'T KNOW HOW TO LAUGH EITHER."

GOLDA MEIR

Me rope be t'eifed. Him t'eifed it. It da be gawn!" Cassandra howled loudly, tears wetting her sweet brown cheeks.

I ran to her, knelt on the dusty road, and took her firmly by the shoulders. "Cassandra, look at me," I commanded. "Tell me what is wrong."

I was in southern Belize working with my husband to reopen a long-closed clinic for women. We rented a simple concrete block-house on a quiet dirt street near the edge of town, an area locals referred to as "outback."

Seven-year-old Cassandra lived next door in a rumbled clap-board shack with three younger siblings, a teenage aunt and uncle, and her grandmother, who she called Granny. Her mother lived and worked in the distant Belize City and sent money home to Granny every month. This arrangement wasn't unusual in Belize. Mothers and fathers had to go to where there was work.

It was a bumpy, ill-maintained road that connected the Toledo District to the rest of the country. Although buses ran back and forth daily between Belize City and Punta Gorda Village, it was a long, dusty eight-hour ride in the dry season; a risky fifteen to twenty-four hours during the wet. Travel was discouraging for Belizeans and tourists alike. Cassandra's mother visited only once during the six months I lived next door. Granny raised the children alone.

As I took Cassandra by the shoulders, she raised her face toward the sky and bared her teeth. A primal groan came from behind her clenched teeth, low and guttural at first, then rose to a shrill crescendo as she opened her mouth widely and screamed.

I pulled her close to me and felt her fragile bird-like ribs as I hugged her gently. Cassandra wrapped her skinny little arms around my shoulders and clung like a spider monkey while she sobbed into my neck. I stroked her back. *What on earth is it? Cassandra—the one with the big smile and a happy squeal. She's the one I call Sunshine. What could be wrong?*

I noticed Junior, the five-year-old old brother, sitting at the road's edge with downcast eyes.

"Junior, what is wrong with Cassandra?" I asked.

"Him t'eifed it. Da boy, he t'eifed da rope," he mumbled just as Cassandra released another scream.

"What? I don't understand. What happened?" I asked again, shouting to be heard over her cries.

"Da boy, he t'eifed da rope," he muttered again a little louder.

I often had trouble understanding the children when they spoke. Although English is the official language of Belize, it is a fascinating country with several unique ethnic groups—Creole, East Indian, Mopan Mayan, Qui'chi Mayan, Mestiszo, and Garifuna. Each has mingled their original language with English and created their own Pidgin version.

These children were Garifuna. Their ancestors came from the fusion of two cultures when several slave ships sailing from Africa wrecked off the coast of the island of Saint Vincent. The slaves that swam ashore joined with the Arawak Indians. The blending of these two cultures created the unique clan of the Garifuna—the "Black Carib."

Both cultures had a long history of skillful canoe building and the art of fishing. Eventually, many settled up and down the coast of Central America in small villages where fishing continues to be their way of life. Punta Gorda was one of those villages.

Cassandra continued to wail while as we rocked back and forth. I whispered, "Shh, shh. It's going to be all right," over and over, until her sobs began to subside. Pulling away, I lifted the tail of my skirt to her nose and instructed her to blow. She did, then gave one last shudder and was still.

"Your jump rope has been taken?" I asked. She nodded sadly with downcast eyes. "Da, me rope it be t'eifed," she answered in a hollow voice.

The children in the run-down little shanty had no toys save that six-foot length of twisted hemp with knots tied at the ends. They made their own fun using little more than their imaginations. Cassandra's jump rope was the only toy I'd seen them play with since I moved in next door. It entertained her for hours as she counted how many times she could jump without missing a hop.

Cassandra was driven. She competed against herself. "One day, Miss Nancy, I will jump to one-thousand," she assured me. Every day she set a new goal. Every day she came running down the road to greet me when I returned from my clinic, and I'd say, "Hello, Sunshine, how many jumps today?"

She would giggle and toss her head with just enough attitude to be adorable and announce the number, exaggerating a little, I was certain. "Three hundred and forty-six," she had proudly announced just yesterday. That was Cassandra, just a scrawny little brown-skinned girl with big, bright eyes and a cocky attitude.

She lived in a weatherworn, unpainted shanty with wooden shutters, but no glass panes or screens on the windows. I didn't know if the family had enough to eat all of the time. I did notice that each of the children seemed hungry whenever I offered food, but that might be said of all children anywhere.

They were a motley looking little gang dressed in rag-tag clothing. They seemed to own few possessions. With only one school uniform each, they ran home each day and changed into play clothes. Cassandra always wore one of three things—a baggy, blue, flowered shift two sizes too big, a yellow dress with one sleeve torn off, or just her white cotton under panties. I suspected the underwear-only days were laundry days.

One afternoon I saw the gang—Julia, Elvin, and Junior—run from the house chasing Cassandra. She stopped in the middle of their tall grassy yard. The others crowded around her like teenage boys around a centerfold.

"What have you got there, Sunshine?" I called across the yard.

All four came running and Cassandra proudly presented the treasure she cradled in her hand—a single peeled hard-boiled egg.

"Dis be fo we," Cassandra said.

I was shaken to understand that the one egg was to be the after-school snack for all four children. The egg disappeared in four bites with Cassandra controlling the bite size with her fingers and threats of, "Yo bite me, I beat yo."

I marveled at her spirit and wondered where this little ironclad angel's will came from. Cassandra was a survivor, just like her great, great, great grandparents. It was coded in her DNA.

The jump rope was her only toy. It entertained, not only her, but also the others—Julia, Junior, and Elvin, who they liked to call "Fat Dog," even though he was as rail thin as the others. Together they used the rope to tie up the enemy in a Belizean version of "Cowboys and Indians," which went more along the lines of "the Brits and the Arowaks." Sometimes, they slung one end of the rope up over a tree branch and swung from the dangling ends like trapeze artists. Now the rope was gone, and with it, my Sunshine's sparkle.

As the sun dropped behind the village in the quiet surrender of evening, I rocked a very sad little girl in my arms. *Tomorrow I'll check at the store to see if they have any rope I can buy for her. I don't want to promise it tonight. These kids have enough disappointments.*

That night, just like every other night, I went to the window when I heard the children calling, "Good night, Miss Nancy." Usually, they all ended their day by singing me a song, but tonight, only the others sang. Cassandra stood quietly, unsmiling, with one elbow propped on the windowsill, her head resting in her palm. She stood alone, staring out into the night as the others went on to bed.

"Good night, Sunshine," I called softly across the few feet between our houses. She raised her hand limply and gave a half-hearted wave, then slowly closed the shutters.

I spent a fitful night punctuated by a child's cries and rooster's crows. It was impossible to separate reality from my dreams. I tossed and turned, awakening frequently. I was incensed. It seemed so unfair that life was playing its twisted tricks against my little friend. That wretched thief had stolen more than just her jump rope. He has stolen her innocence.

I awoke with a start to the sound of Cassandra's shrill scream, but it was only a dream. Shaking it off, I rose from bed and padded to the kitchen for a drink of water. I stood in the pitch-dark kitchen and peered out the window into the abyss of the waning moon. *I wonder if Cassandra is sleeping now. I hope so. She's probably exhausted from all that crying...My little sunshine gal...I wonder who took her rope...and why?*

But, of course, the answer was simple. It could have been any one of the other toy-less children in the village who had taken the rope. Poverty doesn't intrinsically build strong character or respect for boundaries. In fact, it may do quite the opposite. In a struggle where only the fittest survive, competition is the every essence of existence. Sadly, some children learned early to take what they didn't have from those who did. Feelings of jealousy bubbled up until even something as simple as a hank of rope became the object of obsession. Stealing, "t'iefing," as they called it, was common in Punta Gorda.

The next morning I awoke to the jangle of an early alarm. I wanted to be at the grocery store—the one that sold everything from fresh chickens to nails—when they opened. With luck they would have rope.

As I made my way down the road, past Granny's clapboard shanty, I heard a muffled sound. I stopped to listen more closely. It seemed to be coming from behind the shanty. Just as I cleared the corner I saw it was Cassandra.

She was in her backyard singing as she performed her morning ritual of bathing. Bare-bottomed in the morning breeze, she sang softly as she filled the bucket from the hand pump. Straining to raise the bucket high overhead, she drenched herself from her nose to her toes. She laughed and squealed as the cold water spilled over her soft, brown skin. She picked up a bar of homemade soap. In no time at all she whipped it into lather and covered herself in a frothy cocoon. And all the while she smiled and sang softly.

I stepped backwards, shielding myself from her view behind a giant bush. I marveled that this happy singing nymph was the same creature who, only the evening before, had keened as though her soul had been splintered.

She sang louder. It was a native song, I thought, since I didn't recognize the words. As she sang she danced in circles, then refilled the bucket by pumping her little arms to the beat of her own music. When the bucket was full, she strained to lift it high overhead and drenched herself again, sending foamy rivulets down her skinny little frame that streamed down her long legs and onto the ground. This time she ended the motion by putting the empty bucket on her head. This freed her arms to join in the dance, and boogie she did to her own drumbeat! She ended the performance by flinging the bucket across the grass and raising her arms skyward as if greeting the sun.

That was Cassandra. Pure sunshine. Resilient as a rubber ball and near to bursting with sass and sparkle. She brought all of life to the forefront of her awareness. She experienced every joy, every sorrow, to the very marrow of her bones.

Cassandra's song ended. She dropped her arms and stopped, panting to catch her breath. Then she spied me hiding behind the bush. "Good Day, Miss Nancy," she called out, white teeth sparkling. "It be a bright new day."

MARIA GABRIEL

"THE LAST OF HUMAN FREEDOMS IS TO CHOOSE ONE'S ATTITUDE."

VICTOR FRANKEL

"Maria Gabriel. Now there was a book with a lot more heat than her jacket implied. At first glance she appeared to be the perfect little wife. Pleasant and poised, she circled the room on her husband's arm, greeting each of us with the customary kiss-kiss into the air while touching gently cheek to cheek. I'd been in Guatemala City for only a few days, but already I knew this was the appropriate way to greet and to say good-bye.

Guatemala surprised me. I came with the baggage of stereotype, expecting a country where the men always led and the women followed. I was surprised by the free discussion of differences between the husband and wife, on equal ground, that occurred in the home I stayed, but that was just one couple and in private. It would be interesting to see the dynamics at this party among the elite of Guatemala City.

It was obvious Maria Gabriel was gentry. She passed through the room with dignity, but whenever addressed, she lowered her eyes and deferred to her husband, Roberto, a tall, distinguished-looking man with broad shoulders and enough gray at the temples to be attractive.

There is a cultural expectation in Guatemala that the man is the head of the house; however, Roberto seemed to carry the concept to an extreme. He treated his wife as if she were a beautiful child on display her role, "to be seen, but not heard."

She was stylishly dressed for the afternoon party. Smooth white pants gloved her long legs like a protective skin. She floated atop three-inch heels. A red jersey peeked from beneath the vivid red, orange, and pink woven shawl she wore wrapped around her upper body in an elaborate knotting, one end thrown over a shoulder. She wore no makeup, and her hair was drawn back in a smooth bun.

As the party wore on, I noticed that Roberto had what I considered an annoying habit. He spoke for his wife, even when a question was directed to her. Like the good Latina wife she was, Maria Gabriel would merely smile and nod in agreement as he spoke. Soon she blended into the scenery, stiff and inanimate as the mahogany chair she sat on.

After dinner the men retired to the patio to smoke cigars and talk about whatever it is men talk about when they are alone together. Having the luxury of servants, Sarah simply led the women into the living room while two browned-skinned, tiny women silently cleared the table.

The room was large and elegant, with a high ceiling and ceramic-tiled floor. The clickety-click of the women's stilettos echoed as we entered. The women relaxed into the two long couches that lined opposite walls. Maria Gabriel chose a straight-back chair off to one side, hands folded primly in her lap.

Soon we were talking and laughing in that camaraderie only women know, switching the conversation to English, because I speak only a little Spanish. I felt the gentle hug of sisterhood snuggle my shoulders like a warm *huipile,* an elaborate embroidered shawl, each village having its own distinctive design that is handed down from one generation to the next. In contrast to the lively warmth of the other women, Maria Gabriel remained subdued, even away from Roberto's watchful eye.

During a comfortable conversation, Marcella volunteered she "felt slapped in the face" whenever a traveler from the Unites States referred to themselves as an American. "What do they think?" she spat. "Am I not an American too?"

All of the women agreed. "We are Americans too," Maria Olga said. "Central Americans."

I was dumbstruck. Never had I given any thought that my description of myself as an American might be offensive; however, in hindsight, it seemed perfectly sensible. I cringed as I remembered the calendars in my suitcase bedecked with photo after photo of my America with the word in large type. They were intended as small gifts for people met along this journey. Sitting red-faced in Sarah's living room, enlightened by six lovely Central American women, I realized my mistake.

Sarah, the hostess, rose and went to the stereo. "We should dance." she announced, "Let's teach Nancy how we dance." The sounds of "The Macarena" filled the room, and panic shot through me like an electrical jolt. I've a malady that's been heard of—two left feet! But, in the face of their enthusiasm, it would have been rude not to join in. Groaning inwardly, I rose to my feet.

What a laugh they had from my stiff attempts. Carmen's mother, Theresa, an octogenarian with silver hair and a cane to match, offered to show me the moves in slow motion. We laughed until our sides ached, but I never felt as if they were making fun of me. It was the kinship of women, connecting in laughter. We shrieked. We howled. We laughed deep down belly laughs that made us gasp and feel alive.

Women need time with other women. It's a natural cycle. As I danced with these women, I felt bold and sensual and sexy. It was just plain fun. I bonded with my American sisters as we laughed, at me and with me, until tears rolled down our cheeks.

Even Maria Gabriel shed her genteel demeanor. She danced with an openness that surprised me. In the process of dancing her hair unwound from its tight twisted bun. When the music stopped, she removed the remaining hairpins and shook her head until her hair fell in a tangle about her shoulders.

Then she raised one eyebrow to Sarah, who was standing by the stereo preparing to restart the music. At first Sarah appeared surprised, then a salacious smile replaced the question mark on her face. She nodded to Carmen, who stood nearest to the door of the living room that stood open to the foyer and to the cigar-smoking men on the patio beyond. A deep knowing chuckle escaped from Carmen as she stepped to the door and pulled it shut.

Sarah took another CD from the stereo cabinet, placed it in the player, and turned around. Without a word the women formed a wide circle around Maria Gabriel. I joined the circle, too, wondering what was about to happen. The room had a pulse, a vibration that echoed my pounding heart. Intuitively, I knew we were on the edge of something wild.

Maria Gabriel slowly loosened her shawl until it draped around her long, elegant neck. Sarah started the music.

The song was vibrant with a primitive beat and unfamiliar words. Whatever it was, the stiff, formal Maria Gabriel was transformed. Slowly at first, she began to remove her shawl with the fluidity of a stripper. As it slid to the floor she danced. Her hips swayed from side to side, then undulated suggestively. Her breasts shimmied; nostrils flared. She danced and danced; her hair became a wild, feral tangle. Her energy built to near zenith, then paused and hovered like a hummingbird, darted in, sucked in the deep nectar, then whisked away in high-energy flight.

The contrast, between the earlier image of a proper, stiff wife and this animated spirit was striking. She was Ixchel, Mayan Goddess of Fertility. She was Diana, Roman protector of all things natural and free. She was a wild-woman. She was every woman.

We clapped and cheered; our circle pulsated with her to the beat.

There is a spark in every women's wild soul that can't be smothered. Even oppressed women find ways to express themselves. Sensuality and creativity won't be contained. Roberto may think he controls Maria Gabriel, but he doesn't. Men may think they can control women, but they can't, especially when women support each other in expressing themselves in authentic ways.

Eventually, the music ended, and there we were—The Sisterhood. Just a room full of ordinary American women who gasped for breath and laughed with the joy only women and goddesses can understand.

Maria Gabriel smoothed her hair back into a tight bun at the base of her long, elegant neck. She knotted her shawl modestly around her chest and tossed one end over her shoulder. With eyes still shining, she nodded to Carmen, who opened the door. And seven American women sat quietly down on the couches in polite conversation as the men returned from smoking their cigars on the patio.

THE PEACHES

"WE HAVE TO LAUGH, BECAUSE LAUGHTER, WE ALREADY
KNOW, IS THE FIRST EVIDENCE OF FREEDOM."

ROSARIO-CASTELLNOS

"Oh! Nancy's peaches are de-li-cious!" Nurse Dijetare said, giving her long, black hair a toss, her dark eyes uncharacteristically bright as she drew the word out salaciously and set off a wave of laughter among the quarantined medical team.

I worked in a medical project as part of a large post-war recovery effort in the Balkans. My job was to train Muslim-Albanian nurses and doctors in the basics of prenatal care.

Scattered about the Kosovar countryside were little *ambulantas*—stark, tiny clinics with only the most basic equipment. Throughout the scorching summer, while hot winds howled like mournful hounds through the half-opened windows, we worked together side by side to bring prenatal care into remote areas where the concept of seeing a clinician throughout her pregnancy was as foreign to the village women as this plainspoken American who had just offered up her peaches.

The previous week, one of the doctors came down with Rubella and exposed the entire unvaccinated Kosovar medical team to the disease. Immunizations were just one of the many things unavailable to Albanian people under the harsh Serbian rule prior to the war.

The doctor was sent home to recover, the others put in isolation for three weeks to assure they too did not break out in the red spots that could be so damaging to a growing fetus. Now, instead of spending their days in the villages providing care, they were confined to the office.

The brighter side of the quarantine was, at least it gave us time to spend on training. It seemed odd that an American nurse practitioner would be teaching doctors; however, the alternative education system they had trained under was sorely lacking.

Medical training for the Albanian-Muslim doctors had been thwarted by political unrest over the past twenty years. When the Orthodox Serbians took power in 1981, they forced all Muslims out of government jobs and out of schools. The Albanians developed a separate, underground, parallel system of both medical education and healthcare provision from their Serbian counterparts. They did the best they could under difficult circumstances; however, the young doctors who were educated in this system had large gaps in their training. Prenatal care, for example, was not addressed, but the fact that medical school was taught at all—literally out of homes and garages—was a shining tribute to the strength of spirit, resilience, and tenacity of these wonderful people. But now time and funding were running out. We had only four months left to complete their training.

We sat on hard plastic chairs, crowded around the small picnic table that served as our training center. It was uncomfortable, especially in the afternoon when the hot sun baked through the curtainless window, and the Santa Ana-like winds blew in like an efficient central air system gone awry, blasting hot air into the room.

I invited the women to the house I lived in next door to the office. The heavy gold brocade curtains were tightly drawn to block some of the day's heat. Surely we'd be more comfortable lounging in the living room than sticking to the hot plastic seats in the sweltering office.

The house was provided for humanitarian workers. It was large with four bedrooms upstairs. I spent most of my time working, but late nights I rambled alone in the large, creaky house. Occasionally, however, I was surprised when another worker arrived in the middle of the night. Communication systems didn't work well in Kosovo. Telephones rarely worked, two-way radios sometimes, and even verbal messages often didn't get passed on. More than once I awoke in the middle of the night to the sound of the front door scraping open, voices in the foyer, or soft footsteps on the stairs. Each time, heart pounding, I crept from my bed and peeked out the bedroom and hollered as loud as I could, "Who's there?"

It was always another humanitarian worker, new to Kosovo, or passing through on his or her way to another part of the country, but I never quite got used to the surprise. Even more unnerving were the mornings I woke up to find someone sleeping in the next room or already brewing coffee, and I realized I had slept too deeply to hear them come in.

"Get comfortable. I'll get us something to eat," I said as I led the medical team into the foyer and kicked off my shoes.

Each of the women removed their shoes and began to find a place on one of the long couches at both ends of the long, narrow living room. The nurses, Dijetare and Bedrije, sat on one couch; the doctors, Drita and Mirvete on the other. Nurse Hamide sat quietly on the floor.

Although we had worked together only a few weeks, each of the women had shared with me at least part of their personal horror story of war. I was moved by how deep their need to talk about it was—their need to be heard. Without prompting, their sad stories spilled out, usually with tears, but sometimes dry-eyed and detached as if talking about something that had happened to a stranger a long time ago.

Except for Doctor Drita, who was a little older, all the women were in their late twenties or early thirties. They were just children when the Serbians took control of their country and their lives. All of the women carried the invisible weight of depression. It showed in their eyes—the windows to their souls—and in the way they carried themselves, moving lethargically, in slow motion, as if only sheer will made them go about their activities of daily living.

Dijetare, a beautiful young woman in her late twenties, had thick, long, coal black hair she wore loose around her shoulders. She rarely smiled, and when she did, it was a tight, forced effort, like a model made to hold a pose too long. Dijetare's large, brown eyes held a hard history. Her hurt began with her father's death twenty years ago. A writer with unpopular political views, he was beaten and left in the forest with both hands severed. Dijetare was only eight years old.

Bedrije, at twenty-two, was the youngest of the woman. Her blonde hair and blue eyes contrasted with Dijetare's dark, exotic beauty. Bedrije's cheeks dimpled when she spoke, especially when she spoke to the handsome young Conti, one of the young men who served as both driver and guard for the medical team. Bedrije was married—a loveless relationship—arranged early by parents concerned over her free spirit. She rarely mentioned her husband to the other women. Conti, on the other hand, came up often in conversations.

Hamide sat on the green shag carpet, legs crossed in yoga position, under her dark gathered skirt. She sat quietly, not speaking, hands folded in her lap, brown eyes cast down. It was easy to overlook Hamide in a group. She was experienced at being invisible. Her father had died when she was twelve. Her mother married soon after, but because children are considered their father's property, Hamide was sent to live with her paternal grandparents, a stern, serious couple that practiced the older and stricter Muslim ways.

"They are not...um...modern Muslims," Hamide told me earlier in the week as we practiced conversational English. "They were...disciplined. They allowed my mother...only little...visits to me."

Doctor Drita sank down on the far end of one of long brocade couches with a heavy sigh and turned her head away from Doctor Mirvete sitting in the middle of the couch. Drita had a port wine birthmark on the right side of her face; she usually turned it away whenever she spoke. Her face was further disfigured by a flaccid drooping at the left edge of her mouth that caused spittle to gather and roll down her chin if not wiped often with the large white handkerchief she carried in her pocket. Doctor Drita was only in her mid-forties, but she looked at least twenty years older. Life and circumstance had not been kind. Her husband, also a doctor, was killed when they cared for Albanian resistance soldiers. Doctor Drita's life was spared, but she wore unspeakable scars just the same. She went about her work quietly, talking only when necessary. She rarely smiled; however, when she did, her entire face opened up. Drita had an incredible depth of spirit. When she spoke of her losses, it was usually in terms of how losing their father affected her children, a son, age thirteen, and a daughter, eleven.

Doctor Mirvete, a large-boned woman with solemn, dark eyes and short, black hair translated for Hamide and Drita, who spoke less English than the others. She explained I was getting us something to eat. Mirvete often took a leading role with the group; she particularly liked to tell the younger nurses what they should do. She was instructing Bedrije to "go help Nancy in the kitchen" when I walked through the doorway from the kitchen carrying a tray of fresh fruits and cheese.

At the market the day before I was amazed at the variety of fresh fruits and vegetables, as well as other things laid out on tables under red and blue tarp tents. There had been everything from fresh, plump, red-skinned ripe tomatoes to piles of dull yellow chicken's feet bleeding from their severed ankles. I could have purchased a knock-off Rolex watch or a live turkey, but instead left the market with a bag filled with only vegetable and fruits. What I was most excited about were the peaches—wonderful, ripe, luscious peaches that hadn't been available on earlier market days.

I offered the tray to the nurses and doctors and said, "You've just got to try my peaches. They are delicious!"

My remark caused an uproar among the women. It began with only Bedrije snickering and nudging Dijetare in the ribs. Dijetare began to giggle, and then the entire group of women sitting on both couches began to laugh.

Nurse Bedrije and Doctor Mirvete both spoke English very well. They kept repeating, "Try my peaches. Try my peaches. They are de-li-cious," and laughing until tears rolled down their checks. Nurse Dijetare translated for Hamide and Drita, who didn't understand at first; however, once translated they, too, began howling in laughter.

"What? What did I say?" I asked as I laughed with them. I could tell from the sort of laughter it was and from the tone of their voices as they chattered among each other in Albanian that I had made some sort of faux pas.

They other women continued to howl and exchange remarks about "Nancy's delicious peaches."

It felt good to see the smiles on their dark faces—faces that were usually held in tight masks. Their dark, sad eyes had all viewed scenes no one should ever have to see. I'd been with them for a few weeks and rarely saw them smile. The only other time I had heard their laughter was when we were frightened by a turtle we mistook for a landmine on the road. Hard times and horror had been part of these women's daily life. It showed in their eyes and in their hesitant manner. They each carried scars, cauterized deep into her body memory.

"Come on. Come on. Help me out. What did I say?" I begged. I didn't really care if they were laughing at me. It was so good just to hear them laugh.

Hamide was just beginning to study the English language. Sometimes in the evening she stayed after the others left and we practiced simple conversations. Only the night before she taught me a touching sentence. *Kam shprese*. It means, "I have hope." Now she enjoyed teasing her teacher.

"Miss Nancy, how many peaches…you do have?" Little Hamide asked.

"Good sentence, Hamide!" I replied. I counted the fruit on the tray. "It looks like I have five."

This set the group into hysterics. They laughed so hard they could barely talk; Nurse Dijetare translated what I had said for Doctor Drita, who then laughed so hard she nearly wet herself as she ran for the bathroom.

"Are you guys going to tell me what it means?" I asked again just as Doctor Drita returned from the bathroom. Drita said something in Albanian to Bedrije. She seemed to be saying they should include the American in the joke.

"No! Not me! Dijetare, tell her," Bedrije said, laughing as she passed the buck to her friend.

"No! Hamide, you tell her," Dijetare replied, covering her face with her hands.

"No! No me! Doctor Mirvete," little Hamide shrieked, cheeks braising red.

Doctor Mirvete just shook her head and continued to howl.

Finally, blushing through her laughter as she wiped her tears away, Bedrije said, "Miss Nancy, in our country we call the word 'peaches' . . ." Then she covered her face with one hand and pointed to her crotch with the other, sending the group into another spasm of laughter.

It was a good joke on me. I laughed along with the other women until finally, gasping for breath, I managed to say, "Oh, I guess then I only have one," which sent everyone into another laughing fit.

I was awed by these women's strength. They each had lived through their own private hell, before and during the war, but now they persistently worked to rebuild their lives and their country.

And the fact that they could howl with laughter together on this hot afternoon gave me hope that maybe, just maybe, both they, and their country, could begin to heal. I heard little Hamide's voice in my head whisper...*Hope is life. Life is hope. Kam shprese.* I have hope.

Dance, Baby Girl, Dance

"Unusual travel suggestions are dancing lessons from God."

Kurt Vonnegut

It was the rainy season in the Kingdom of Tonga—the messy season. My seventy-seven-year-old white-haired mother and I had arrived in this island country, east of Fiji and South Samoa, only the day before. It took twenty-four hours to get there from Midwestern America. The purpose of the journey: a visit to my daughter, Shannon, a Peace Corps volunteer.

Travel is always about going from where you are to another place. On a higher plane, it is about expanding your awareness. I have traveled to many exotic places in the world and have experienced many grand adventures; however, nothing compares to learning about yourself through the eyes of your mother and daughter. I had no idea how much I would learn along this journey about our relationships.

Initially, I hadn't wanted to bring Mom along. My mother is a refined lady, used to many amenities in her life; her idea of exotic travel was to stay in an upscale hotel and take a taxi wherever she went. I thought Mom had no idea what she was getting into, and the responsibility of taking care of a frail septuagenarian in a Third World country daunted me. Selfishly, I feared she would slow me down, and I'd end up spending all my time looking after her when the primitive living conditions wore her out, or worse, made her sick. I tried to paint an accurate picture of how different Tonga was from the United States, but Mom was adamant.

"I want to go," she said firmly with a stubborn set to her jaw.

I knew that look all too well. When Mom makes up her mind, there's no changing it. Besides, how could I tell my own mother "no," especially with her so proud of those bright, flowered kaftans she had sewn for us to wear on the island?

I foresaw challenges brewing, but the picture in my mind of the three of us sitting around a mahogany table dressed like a three-generation triplets act in bright pink, blue, and purple kaftans, sipping rum drinks from coconuts with little umbrellas did make me smile. Mothers and daughters, such tangled, braided lives we lead. I tried to put a positive spin on the trip. Three wild woman dancing life's dance on a tropical island. It would be fun, wouldn't it?

Just six months earlier, Shannon had excitedly telephoned. "Mom! I got my assignment! I'm going to Tonga!"

Geographically challenged, I blankly replied, "Tonga? Is that in Africa?"

"No, Mom." I could picture Shannon's eyes rolling in that all too familiar way, a gesture that began around age six when Shannon, with an IQ near genius, began to realize that she was smarter than her mother. "The South Pacific. Can you believe it! I'm going to an island kingdom in the middle of the South Pacific!"

Her enthusiasm was unmistakable and contagious. She would live out her childhood aspiration. She wanted this since age twelve. I felt a stab of pride mingled with a pinch of regret and envy. Unknowingly, she was living my own unmet dream as well. Shannon had joined the Peace Corps, something I would have done had not a baby arrived before my college degree. Now, somewhere west of the United States, in the middle of the Pacific Ocean, she would live and work for the next two years. She didn't know yet what her work would involve but, being a linguistics major, assumed it would have something to do with languages.

The first letter arrived shortly after she left for Tonga. Her work was largely teaching English as a Second Language to school-aged children. She was given only a nine-week course in the Tongan language. Luckily, Shannon picked up the language quickly and soon conversed with everyone in Tongan, a language with only eighteen letters and words like *Malo e' leli* (Hello) and *A'lu ki fei?* (How are you?)

She taught two groups of young people who didn't necessarily see the value of learning a language not needed to live in their country. Everyone speaks Tongan. English is their second official language, but it is used only in positions of prestige. In the Tongan culture, role is a very complicated issue based on status, and it is nearly impossible to rise above the rank into which you are born. The young people recognized that they had no chance of upward mobility, thus had no basis for motivation to learn a language they would never use.

The Tongans have a word for white-skinned people—*palangi*. A few students were eager learners, working hard and ever ready to please their white-skinned, green-eyed *palangi* teacher. Others challenged her daily with their lackadaisical attitudes, their defiance passive-aggressive. Rather than blatantly defying her, they acted sullen and stubborn. They twittered in Tongan among themselves, recognizing that she understood only part of what they were saying. They pretended to cooperate, then ran off and left school for days on end.

Shannon had to prepare students to sit for a huge annual test. No one in the administration had any real interest in them actually learning. She was instructed to teach to the test. Shannon found herself caught in the clash between administrators, the principal and the vice-principal, who were from two different families who'd had a long and hateful feud.

Teaching in a school without textbooks in a large gymnasium-sized room without walls to separate the classrooms was hard. Teaching children who had little motivation to learn was even harder. Teaching children without support from administration—the hardest.

The vice-principal insisted she discipline the children like all the other teachers did with severe whacks to the back of the hands or worse—beatings. Shannon balked. Corporal punishment went against everything she believed in for children. The thought of beating a child made her stomach turn and made her toss and turn all night. She wanted to work within the culture, to respect the principal's suggestions, and bend to the local mores; however, to beat a child was terribly wrong. She couldn't do it. No, she would find another way. By defying the principal she made an enemy, a very powerful enemy. She couldn't count on support from his office again.

But the angst from some of her students was only part of the strain of living in this strange country. Machismo and a general disrespect for women ran rampant. Even law enforcement didn't take crimes against women seriously. Two Peace Corps volunteers had been raped since Shannon arrived in the country. No arrests were made. Everyone simply looked the other way.

Shannon traveled to Europe several times during high school and college. After graduation from University of Kansas, she taught English in Chiapas, Mexico. But even for a well-traveled young woman, adapting to this new culture was a challenge. She wrote, telephoned, or e-mailed whenever possible. Her communications seemed filled with increasing nervous tension and depressed thoughts.

So, Mama and Grandma—who's connection to Shannon is nearly as close as my own—flew across the country and the ocean to wrap our arms around our young and reassure her, if not with our presence, at least with presents—large suitcases filled with chocolate, cream-soup mixes, and other comfort foods. That is what brought us to the island of Tongatapu located in the heart of the South Pacific.

As our plane circled round the small runway and began its sharp descent, Mom peered out the window and watched the palm trees grow from tiny miniatures to huge real-sized.

"So, this is where she lives," Mom remarked. "She's sure a long way from home."

"She sure is," I replied.

We gathered our carry-on baggage and departed the plane. We proceeded through Customs for a rather casual and cursory inspection of our luggage by a huge uniformed man wearing a blue skirt and a tan shirt that fit so tightly the buttons were near to bursting against his large chest.

Shannon waited for us inside the airport. When I first spied her, I gasped. Throughout her adolescence, Shannon's naturally curly hair hung down her back to her waist. During college, she chose a smart, shorter, shoulder-length bob. However, inside the Tongan airport Shannon stood wearing a long skirt and a *kiekie*, a woven belt with braided pieces hanging from it that looked like an over-skirt. But it wasn't her *kiekie* that caught my attention. It was her hair cut in a crew-cut style! I was taken with how much she favored her cousin, Carl.

I immediately began doing what mothers do. I looked for signs of happiness. I looked for signs of worry, my radar on high alert. Shannon looked tired and drawn. She had dark circles under her eyes that suggested she wasn't sleeping well. I had been mildly concerned before. Now I became truly troubled.

We retrieved our luggage and loaded everything into a taxi. As we drove down the muddy road, passing palm trees and concrete homes toward her house, Shannon explained her hair.

"I got lice—yuck—three times! I decided this was just the easiest way to go," she said nonchalantly. Mom and I tried to be positive.

"It looks easy to take care of," I said.

"You've got the eyes to pull it off," said Mom, patting Shannon's leg.

We both thought she looked like a refugee or someone who took military life very seriously, but we couldn't say that out loud. And it was only hair. It would grow. I was more concerned about the weary look in her eyes.

The next morning we made our way through the quagmire between the porch and the side road. It had rained gently, but steadily, throughout the night. The soil, an equal mixture of clay and sand, oozed around our shoes. By the time we reached the main road our feet had swollen two sizes. We wiped our feet as best we could on the grasses at the side of the road and hailed a taxi.

"Hello, Noni," the driver greeted Shannon. She explained to us that was her Tongan nickname. Shannon chatted with the driver in Tongan, the words full of clicking sounds.

Once in town, we scraped the muck off our shoes on the edges of the sidewalk before entering any building. My mother, the ever well dressed peacock, lamented her ruined muck-covered sandals.

"Just look at my shoes and my nails are ruined too," she exclaimed.

Shannon and I just smiled. Our flip-flops would wash off easily enough and, maybe, Grandma would soon learn that coordinating shoes, pedicures, and a modern sense of fashion aren't the most important things when traveling.

We separated in the open-air market, agreeing to meet under the huge tree outside in one hour. We mingled with shoppers and vendors selling every size and shape of root crop you can imagine. We were each in search of our own treasures. Shannon looked for fresh vegetables, surprisingly scarce on the island, save the root vegetables. Mom and I hunted for trinkets to take home. I admired the hand-woven baskets and things made from *Tapa*, a paper-like cloth made from pounded mulberry bark and painted with natural dye.

For eons Tongans have measured their wealth in *Tapa*. *Tapa* is made from bark, pulled off a Mulberry tree, and pounded for hours with a wooden mallet until thin and paper-like. Next, the pounded sheets are glued together with tapioca paste and made into huge room-sized rugs. When they are completely dry, they are painted with traditional and geometric designs using natural dyes. The larger and more *Tapa* rugs you own, the richer you are considered to be.

I hovered over Mom in the market trying to make sure she didn't get trampled. There's a different perception of personal space in Tonga than we are accustomed to in the States. Shannon had explained to us that it was not considered rude in Tonga to push someone out of your way. It was simply a cultural difference, another way of being.

One very large woman body-slammed into me and continued on her way, seemingly unaware that she had nearly knocked me to the ground. I tried to shield my little white-haired osteoporitic mother from the most aggressive shoppers and hurried her through her shopping. I wanted to get her out of the market before she got flattened. As soon as she made her purchases, I led her outside to the large hardwood tree with a concrete abutment around it and sat her down.

"Stay here, Mom," I said. "I'll be back as soon as I can."

I returned to the market where I spied a caramel-skinned little girl, about eight years old, with sad brown eyes and a shy smile, selling yellow leis from a large woven basket. When I asked for "three" and held up fingers to indicate the number, her eyes brightened and broad grin spread over her face.

"My mother will be so proud," she said.

Such a universal wish of all women—to make our mothers proud.

I complimented her English. "You speak English very well."

"Thank you. I learn in school," she replied.

I saw the light in a little girl's eyes brighten from the compliment. I felt proud myself knowing it was probably my daughter who taught this little girl her English.

The most fundamental relationship women have is with their mother. I imagined the little girl did make her mother proud and wondered how often she realized it. How often did I make my own mother proud? Did my daughters realize how proud I was of them? I hoped they did.

Later, I met up with Mom and Shannon at the tree just outside the market. I insisted on getting a picture of our trio—Three Wild Women—necks ringed in yellow bouquets and those six potent words whispering in my head...*my mother will be so proud.*

I spent the next two weeks sandwiched between my perceived needs of my mother and my daughter. And I fretted. I fretted about my daughter's emotional and physical health. She seemed strung tight as a guy-wire ready to snap. She was pale and seemed tired. So, I tried to feed her—everything. Convinced if I could get enough good food into her that her rosy cheeks and sense of humor would return, I smothered my grown daughter.

Shannon and I have always been close from the moment she came screaming into the world and I literally caught her myself as she spilled between my legs and onto the hospital bed. The Labor Ward was exceptionally busy that day, and my nurse didn't believe my shouts, "The baby's coming! The baby's coming now!"

She was a scrawny little thing with huge blue eyes. Arriving six weeks early, her back was covered with black downy fuzz, *lanugo*, giving her the resemblance of a little spider monkey, but I thought she was beautiful.

From the beginning Shan and I seemed to have an uncommon connection. I awakened seconds before she began to cry. Later, as Shannon grew up, we often joked about "sharing one brain." No one allowed us to be on the same team when the family played games like Charades or Pictionary. Shan and I had the unfair advantage. One line drawn and she would shout out, "Walking the dog," or something similar. It was uncanny how we seemed to know the other's thinking.

Perhaps, because of our special connectedness I felt acutely anxious; perhaps, I was simply being a mom. Even though I knew I was driving my daughter crazy with my hovering, I couldn't stop.

I fretted. I fussed.

Shannon chafed.

The Kingdom of Tonga is a country of 176 islands—thirty-six of them inhabited. We had been on the island of Tongatapu, in the city of Nuku'a lofa, for two weeks when Shannon suggested that we fly to one of the smaller islands.

"If you really want to see Tonga, we should go to 'Eua," Shannon said. "The volunteers on the smaller islands really have it rough. I've got it easy in the city compared to what some of them have to live with," she warned.

"I'm game," said Mom. "I want to see it all."

Nukalufa was primitive in comparison to any city in the United States, but at least Shannon's home had running water and electricity most of the time. 'Eua would be much more primitive. I was not certain Mom was up to it. My fret factor soared.

"I'm not sure it's such a good idea," I said

"Oh, Nancy, stop your fussing. I'll be all right. I want to do it. I want to see it all," Mom answered.

"Let's go!" said Shannon.

The following morning we were up before the sun to get to the airport. When we arrived at the small airport, we sat Mom down on a bench to watch our bags. Shannon and I wandered inside to check on our plane.

The young man behind the counter chatted with Shannon in Tongan. I heard him call her Noni and assumed they were friends.

"The plane's on time," she said. She appeared to ask the young man a question, then walked around the counter and stepped onto the scale intended to weigh baggage. I assumed she wanted to weigh herself and, since she had no bathroom scale in her home, had asked her friend if she might use the airport scale. The meter to the scale was on the counter in front of me and out of Shannon's line of vision.

"Seventy kilos," I announced.

If looks could kill, I would have dropped to the floor. Shannon shot daggers at me as she jumped quickly off the scale.

"Your turn, Mom," she glowered.

Confused, and still not understanding my mistake, I declined. "No thanks. I don't want to know what I weigh," I said.

"You don't get a choice, Mom," said Shannon. "It's so they can make sure the plane isn't overloaded."

"You're kidding, right?"

Shannon just smiled an evil little smirk and shook her head. And as I reluctantly climbed on the scale, she announced my weight loudly for me, her friend, and anyone within earshot. I'm thinking it was a sweet moment for my daughter.

We arrived on 'Eua in a mere eight minutes. The plane ascended, then immediately descended onto the tiny island. Lori waited at the airport with a friend who drove a pick-up truck with a bench in the back. Welcome to Tongan tourism, 'Eua style. We climbed into the back and set off to explore the island.

Although it's on the completely opposite side of the world, 'Eua reminded me of southern Belize—only cleaner. Chickens and pigs roamed the streets but must have been eating natural things, as there was no noticeable garbage. Coconut trees swayed in the breeze and plenty of lush green, bright yellow, and purple underbrush reminded me of plants that I had kept as houseplants.

In November the weather, warm and humid but was not unbearably hot. I didn't notice an abundance of flying insects that bite.

"Keep your eye out for the *molakao*," Shannon warned. "He's a huge and ugly centipede that makes you really sick if he bites you with his prehistoric-looking incisors."

Luckily, Mom and I didn't see any *molakao* while we were on 'Eua. We did keep a close watch.

We bounced around in the back of the truck. Although we tried to get Mom to ride inside, she insisted on staying with us.

"Will you just quit worrying about me?" she snapped when I suggested that she ride inside the cab. I finally realized I'd gone too far and retreated but continued to stew inwardly.

She just doesn't understand how worried I am…how worried she should be…what if she gets hurt? What the heck are we doing here? Is there even a doctor on this island?

But Mom did seem happy. Her head was a swivel as she looked from side to side at the scenery and exclaimed, "Isn't this something!"

When we stopped for gas, Mom talked to two little rag-a-muffin children, a boy and a girl, standing on the side of the road. The children didn't speak English, but that didn't stop my mother from chatting away to them, seemingly oblivious that they couldn't understand a word she was saying. Smiles are universal, and I think the children enjoyed her attention; either that or they were struck speechless out of fear.

All the children of 'Eua stared at my mother with wide eyes. Light-skinned people were rare in Tonga and, except for Peace Corp volunteers, practically nonexistent.

"Grandma, they think you're a ghost," Shannon teased.

"Do you really think so?" Mom asked.

"Maybe," Shannon said. "For folks who believe in taboo—the belief that you are safe from your enemies if you hide in the grave-yard—I think seeing you must make them wonder. A white-haired, white-skinned woman must be a ghost!"

"Well, isn't that something," Mom said, smiling. She obviously got a kick out of the idea.

While on our truck tour, I continued to worry about my mother. She suffered several broken bones a few years before, prior to beginning medication for osteoporosis. What if she broke a bone while on 'Eua? But our afternoon adventure tour from the back of a pickup truck was the most fun she'd had in years, or so she said.

"I never thought I'd get to see something like this in my life," she remarked.

After several hours of touring the island, we returned to Lori's house, an unpainted concrete structure without windows, for the night. Just as Shannon had warned, living conditions on 'Eua were much more simple than on the main island. Lori's house had no furniture, save a single twin-sized bed draped with mosquito net-ting. We sat on the mat-covered floor. I felt sorry for Mom as she gently lowered herself to the mat then squirmed to find a comfortable position. We slept on the floor; however, Lori generously gave up her bed to my mother.

And although she was tired and on her way to bed before it was even dark outside, Mom wasn't about to give up her beauty regime. She sat on the edge of the bed brushing her hair and applying moisturizer to her face.

I stood in the doorway and watched. Seventy-seven years old and Mom had not complained one time during our entire visit in Tonga. She bounced around in the back of a pick-up truck all day and never once protested. She sat on the hard floor without the slightest objection. I had been afraid that Tonga would be too much for her, but Mom was a trooper. All afternoon, every time Shannon or I suggested that we return to the house, Mom said, "No, let's see it all!"

Although she looked pale without her makeup, and I knew all that jostling in the truck would probably exact its toll by tomorrow, tonight she looked absolutely radiant.

"Good night, Mom," I said. "You know you are amazing?"

Mom glowed. "We're doing it all, aren't we?" she said with a smile.

We awakened to the clang of the alarm. Groan. It had been a long night. Water was scarce on ʻEua, so we did *mohe uli*; we "slept dirty" and went to bed without washing even our feet. Every time I woke up in the night I felt something crawling on me—probably wee-wee ants. They were everywhere. I was just grateful they were only ants and not the *molakao*.

Mom, Shannon, and I had been together for almost three weeks. Like all mothers and daughters, the complications of our relationships were beginning to wear thin. We started to get on each other nerves. Both Mom and Shan were tired of my sheltering. They formed an alliance that felt like it was them against me. I didn't know what was coming, but a traditional Tongan feast called an *Umu* on the island of ʻEua turned out to be payback.

I woke myself up with an ice-cold spit bath and dressed. The sun was already beating down on our heads as we made our way down the dirt road. The singing had begun as we entered and found our place on a middle pew. Loud singing. So loud we could feel our cochlea vibrating.

The minister was dressed in a traditional *ta'ovala*, a mat tied on with a rope and worn over his *tupenu*, a long wraparound skirt tied at the waist and a western style, long-sleeved cotton shirt. He began to boom his message. Thunderous. Passionate. After the sermon, there was more singing. Voices lifted up until the walls vibrated.

After church we were invited into the minister's home for an *Umu*, a special traditional feast prepared in an underground oven. As was the custom, we removed our shoes before we entered his home. His grown daughter, a pretty woman in her twenties with long, black hair, busily moved the floor mats to be in the appropriate places for us to sit. And sit we did, on the floor. It seemed Lori wasn't the only one on 'Eua who lacked furniture.

Cartoon and movie posters comprised the art on the walls of the room. Batman & Robin and that fellow from "Firestorm" stared down at us from the walls. Western movies, seen only by video, were very popular everywhere in Tonga; in fact, Shannon had told me earlier that videos were probably the best gift that I could send back as a thank you to our new Tongan friends when I returned home to the States.

The meal was interesting. I said *interesting*, not tasty. We were served large portions of *Lu*—sheep's gristle wrapped in a taro leaf and cooked underground in coconut milk. The leaf was the best part. The end result was a slimy, mucous-like texture that made each bite stick halfway down my throat and try to retch back up.

With my first bite I looked toward Shannon in alarm. Shan just winked. Somehow I managed to swallow it and, not wanting to offend our host, managed to clean my plate. Mom simply pushed the food around her plate and apologized to our host for her poor appetite. Later, when bowls were passed for "seconds," Shannon heaped a large scoop of *Lu* onto my plate against my protests. Shannon and Mom exchanged a knowing glance. I think it might have been payback for all my hovering and fretting over the two of them. They enjoyed my discomfort over second portions of *Lu* more than a little bit, while I had visions of projectile vomiting across the room to the wall directly in front of me and splaying *Lu* across the Walt Disney "The Toaster That Ran Away" poster.

The rest of the dinner was easier on the palate. We ate yams by the hunk, as well as tapioca. Both were bland and slid down easily when chased with a shot of *Otia*—coconut milk mixed with watermelon.

As we left the minister's home and walked up the muddy road toward Lori's house, Mom elbowed me gently in the side. "Did you get enough to eat?" she asked. Shannon laughed out loud.

Paybacks are hard.

The following morning we repeated the short flight back to the main island. Shannon needed to return to work. It was nearly time for Mom and me to return home.

On our last night in Tonga, we took a long taxi ride to the other end of the island for a huge buffet and a dance show. We watched the sun sink into the horizon to an eclectic blend of music that had a Polynesian flavor but with tunes like "Take Me Home West Virginia" mixed in as well. It was a strange combination. I felt as though I were in some sort of South Seas twilight zone. It occurred to me that Shannon was living in a surreal world. *How could I possibly think that I could accurately evaluate her emotional condition in this unreal place? Could it be that some of the angst and anxiety I felt was actually my own boomeranging back at me?*

Shan chatted and visited with her friends. "*Malo e' lelei, Noni, 'alu Kifer?*" (Hello, Noni. Where are you going?) Greetings came from so many people that it seemed she knew almost everyone on the island. *Why did I feel she was all alone? It was easy to see she had lots of friends.*

A dance show followed dinner. Oiled bodies of young men and women writhing and gyrating to the drumbeat of ancient rhythms coded in their DNA. There were both men and women dancers; however, they performed separately.

The men pounded the floor with their spears during the Club Dance—a ferocious dance, something akin to a war chant or the threatening roar of a lion challenging the alpha male of a pride. Fierce. Threatening. Loud. Men with smooth caramel-colored skin and well-developed muscles dressed in green, palm-fronds over brightly colored *tupenus,* the traditional wraparound skirt worn by most adult males, danced to the ever-increasing beat of the drums. They each held a thick stick made of mahogany, flattened on one end forming a thin club and pointed on the other like a spear. These "clubs" were incorporated into the dance with plenty of whirling about, faster and faster, underscored with fierce pounding and punctuated by thunderous feral grunts.

Next, groups of mild mannered, dark-eyed women wearing red and green grass skirts and tight-fitting *Tapa* bodices danced gracefully using their arms and hips in a gentle choreography. One particular dance, the Hand Dance, was performed almost totally with their hands and arms. They sat crossed-legged on the floor and mesmerized us with their gentle, soothing synchronization of the very slow, tranquil dance. The Hand Dance is the Yin to the Club Dance's Yang.

It is custom for the audience to reward the dancers' performance by slapping *pa'anga* bills, Tongan money, on their well-oiled arms, backs, and shoulders while they danced. The dancers didn't acknowledge the dollars being slapped on their bodies. They seemed not even to feel it happen or be distracted by the soft monetary slaps. They simply continued dancing.

The last act of the show was the children. Creamy-skinned little girls dressed in palm frond skirts danced in near perfect harmony. One little girl, six-year-old Mele, the smallest of the dancers, stole the show. She growled at a little boy, slightly bigger than herself, who caught the dollars as they fell off Mele's shoulders and stuffed them down his dancing older sister's blouse instead of saving them for Mele.

Mele scowled her indignant displeasure at the boy, but he only laughed and continued to grab up the falling dollars as she protested. She hissed at him and appeared to try to bite him as she continued to dance. Then, just as she spun around, tiny feet moving to the beat, arms outstretched, little Mele's skirt fell to the floor! The music continued, the beat racing faster and faster, all the dancers continued to smile as they moved about the floor, arms held out gracefully as if no one on stage had noticed little Mele's predicament.

In a brief freeze-framed moment, Mele's mother, sitting in the front row of the audience, made eye contact with her tiny daughter. As she jumped up and took a step toward the dancing little girl, Mele frowned and shook her head fiercely and hissed.

The audience held a collective breath. Empathically, we shared her frustration and embarrassment.

She stood still for a brief moment as if trying to decide what to do. Then she stamped her foot twice, reached down, and yanked her skirt back up covering her tiny belly button, and resumed dancing.

Little Mele got it just right when she pulled up her own skirt and kept dancing. What a wise women, her mother, to stay seated.

On the evening we left Tonga, Shannon taxied with us to the airport, but due to airport security we had to say good-bye outside the gates. I hugged my daughter long and hard and tried to swallow back a sob that welled up in my throat.

"I know, Mom. I love you too," she said. "I'm good, Mom—really good," she added.

And she was good. I arrived in Tonga full of worry and left overwhelmed with pride. My daughter worked a difficult job that was not likely to get easier. I knew she had hard days ahead, as well as wonderful ones. Shannon was making a small difference in the world as she built amazing memories. "Noni" was learning the steps that year to a very complicated Tongan dance of life. She certainly didn't need any lessons from her mother. She simply needed to know that she made her mother proud.

As we settled into our seats on the airplane, Mom remarked, "Well, we did it all, didn't we?"

We sure did, Mom. We did it all.

SECTION TWO

ALL IN HER DAY'S WORK

A Picnic in Hoghoost

"An eye for an eye ends up making the whole world blind."

Mahatma Gandi

I woke to the sound of a dove cooing on the balcony outside my bedroom window. Such a soft, pure sound, although a rather inconsistent symbol in this country so not full of peace. The next sound I heard—the rustling vibration of rats scurrying about in the attic overhead—was probably more congruous with the uneasy tenor of Kosovo.

I gave a loud yawn and a full stretch from the roots of my hair to the tips of my toes. It was a good day, July 3, the eve of my own country's celebration of freedom. I had been in Kosovo for only one month, but long enough to see and hear way more than I was prepared for.

Kosovo has been the backdrop to a centuries old strained relationship between its two primary ethnic groups—Serbians and Albanians. Since 1981, it had been the Serbs in power. They reined havoc on the underdog Albanian's lives. However, the most recent conflict between the groups ended when NATO forces bombed the Serbian Army in the spring of 1999, and put an end to what the press had euphemistically called "ethnic cleansing." Believe me, there was nothing clean about the things that happened in Kosovo during the ten years leading up to NATO's involvement.

Beatings and murders were common, the victims, usually Albanian men, involved in the resistance. Rape was used as an effective method of wielding power over the Muslim-Albanian women. To make matters worse, when a Muslim woman was raped, she was then shunned by her family for the shame she brought to them. Babies who resulted from the rapes were abandoned at birth or killed by their own mothers.

Much of the infrastructure was gone, including many bridges and oil refineries. Many homes and businesses stood as charcoal skeletons of their previous structures, burned out by the Serbian Army. Telephones worked in part of the country, but only part of the time. Education and healthcare were in shambles. Both electricity and water were intermittent. Sometimes, part of the country was without both for days.

Much of rural Kosovo was without adequate shelter. I visited families who lived in shells of burnt-out houses or in tents erected beside where their homes had stood before the war. Many homes lacked running water, and water had to be carried home, jug-by-jug, from a community well.

The countryside was littered with landmines laid by both sides of the conflict. Many farmers were afraid to work their fields due to fear of setting off landmines. Those that did used only hand tools because the Serbian Army had confiscated all farm machinery at the border when farmers tried to flee the country with their valuable equipment.

But now, Kosovo was beginning to heal; or perhaps it's more accurate to say that a scab was forming. The country was officially at peace, but it was a very fragile peace to say the least.

After the conflict officially ended in June 1999, thousands of Serbians fled the country in fear of retaliation. Their fear was well founded. The Albanian-Muslim's have a code of retribution that is part of their religion and their ethnicity. It commands the oldest son in every family avenge ten times over any wrong done to his family. For nearly ten years, it had been the Albanian-Muslims suffering under the hard dictatorship of Serbian rule. They had been treated as second-class citizens and worse. The West intervened and brought an end to a decade of abuses.

And the pendulum swung back. Serbs fled the country by the thousands. Albanians began their revenge. Ten-fold.

Kosovo was full of contrasts. When I first arrived in the country, I was housed just two doors down from Indira Rugova, who was expected to be elected Kosovo's first president. The home neighborhood was upscale, the streets paved. The following week I staffed my first village clinic in a dirty, rundown concrete building without running water. I visited patients' burnt homes and saw families living in conditions that broke my heart.

There was a surreal quality to day-to-day life. One day I walked past a group of men sitting at an outdoor café, drinking coffee, and chatting it up. The next I heard of a drive-by shooting on the very street. Four Serbians were killed.

The following day, just outside of town, four Albanian women were shot as they worked in the field with wooden handmade tools. The concept of retribution, it seemed, was not solely Muslim.

Peacekeepers, the Kosovo Forces, from many countries were in there to maintain the peace. It was the American arm of the Peacekeepers that protected the area where I worked.

One day I went with some American friends to pick up a young Serbian man who needed a ride to the Kosovo Forces (KFOR) base. The young man requested a KFOR escort for his mother. She wanted to return to Serbia, where she had lived since early spring after she was badly beaten in her village and left for dead by a group of Albanian men.

As we rode he talked about what had happened to his family. His eyes filled with tears as he explained to us that his mother had returned today to place the marker on his father's grave, but she did not want to stay even one night in the village after what had happened. His father was killed one year prior by Albanians seeking retribution, but as he said, "Retribution for what? My father was not a political man. It was men that were his friends that killed him. It was the sons of those men who beat my mother."

I think if Kosovo were a painting it would not be bright and colorful; nor would it be clearly black and white, only shades and shades of gray.

Reprisals had been swinging back and forth for centuries. It was discouraging, but I had to hope. Change always occurs in the tiniest of increments. The West had become involved this time in a centuries-old feud. Perhaps, under our influence, the people might begin taking steps toward forgiveness and unity.

The humanitarian workers, along with the Kosovar nurses and

doctors, worked long, hard hours in tiny bare clinics called *ambu-lantas*. However, there was no work for us today. Today we would celebrate America's Independence Day with a picnic in Hoghoost, one of the nearby villages.

We wouldn't be having traditional fireworks, that is not unless the nearby KFOR, the Russian and American soldiers who were there to safeguard the peace, decided to hold one of their pretend attacks they called "illumination rounds." Periodically, they did that. In a show of force, they shot off their guns and lit up the night sky with rounds of ammunition. They just wanted the people, on both sides, Albanian and Serbian, to remember that they were there. It was a reminder to keep the peace. We would have a picnic though, complete with a whole roasted goat, watermelon, and a rousing game of soccer against the villagers of Hoghoost.

Organizing the picnic was no easy feat. Laura, our office coordinator, announced the week before that there would be no work on July 3. In celebration of American's freedom, we would have a picnic.

The process of organizing began. At home in Iowa, potlucks are easy. You just say, "It's a potluck." Everyone brings a dish, and it all seems to work out just fine. I've never been to a potluck where everyone brought the same potato salad or the same plate of fruit. Without any organization, in Midwestern America at least, potlucks seem to have that magical quality of just taking care of themselves.

But nothing happened easily in Kosovo, not even a potluck picnic.

Our staff of doctors, nurses, drivers, and guards was approximately one-third women and two-thirds men. Although daily we worked toward enlightening the Kosovar men about equality between the sexes, even something as innocent as a potluck demonstrated our failure to change their basic mindset.

"The men will give money and the women will make the food," ordered young Conti, reaching into his pocket and bringing out a handful of small *deutschemarks*. As if there were no question about it, the other men began to follow his lead.

Even on the simplest level we took what opportunities presented to point out, or model, equal treatment not only between men and women, but on the larger scale between the two ethnic groups,

Serbian and Albanian as well. Tiny steps—mere centimeters at a time—we hoped to effect change.

"Hold it. Hold it!" said Laura. "No, no, no, we're not going to make it that easy on you men. It isn't fair that you just have to reach in your pocket, but the women have to spend all day cooking." A burst of embarrassed laughter broke out among the group of men.

"How would you women like to do it?" she asked.

In unison all eyes lowered, the women concentrated on an imaginary speck of dirt on the floor. No one spoke.

"Come on," said Laura. "Do you think that it is fair for the men to just pay money, but you have to do all the work?"

"My mother will be happy to cook for us if I only ask her," Sami, a twenty-four-year-old Albanian, who was one of the drivers, smugly interjected. I had previously heard Sami say he would never marry a woman who his mother did not approve, and if he married and his wife did not get along well with his mother, he would divorce her. Where I'm from, Sami would be considered a real mama's boy, but in Kosovo his thinking was not unusual. Albanian men carry the respect for their mothers to a fault, and it is the norm to live in an extended-family situation with the young man's family. As many as four generations may live in the same home, and the young women truly are slaves to their mothers-in-law. In Kosovo it is the mother of the man who wields the power.

Finally, outspoken Bedreji, one of the younger nurses with a more modern view of the world and a spunky attitude, spoke. "It is *not* fair," she said, shaking her blonde curls, blue eyes snapping. "The men must help. They can cook, or they can go to the market and buy something to carry to the picnic, but they cannot just reach into their pockets and be done." She folded her arms determinedly across her chest.

It was a small risk for Bedreji to challenge the men. Traditionally, such an outburst from a women would not be tolerated; however, Bedreji knew she had Laura's support, as well as that of the entire group of humanitarian workers in the room to back her up. Besides, Bedreji was confident and drop-dead gorgeous in a sexy, Marilyn Monroe sort of way. Probably half the young drivers had a crush on her. She knew it, and that knowledge probably made it easier for her to be assertive.

I smiled to myself as the other women nodded but kept their eyes still focused on the ground. Even their little nod of agreement was an indication toward a new way of thinking.

Groans and moans broke out among the men, but it was only good-natured complaining.

"Okay," said Laura, "I thought so. So, now I'm putting a sign-up sheet on the wall, and if you don't sign up by tomorrow for what you want to bring, I'll assign you something."

It was settled. The picnic would be a true potluck. But knowing how change comes in very small increments, mere baby steps, I smiled to myself as I thought, *I wonder what these young men's mothers will cook for us?*

So, that is how our Fourth of July celebration, albeit held on the third, came to be. We gathered in front of the office, a large windowed building, formerly a clothing store, and began loading the vans with plastic tables and chairs and food for the picnic. Each woman brought a casserole or salad. The men, bags of potato chips and sodas—not unlike what one would expect of a potluck in the States.

"I bought these myself," announced one of the drivers as he added his chips to the growing pile of food filling the back of the van. A dimple winked in his left cheek as he asked, "Does this make you happy, Bedreji?"

Bedreji tossed her head flirtatiously and smiled. "Maybe," she responded.

"It makes me happy," Dijetare murmured. "You are becoming a modern man, Xhelal." Dijetare's long eyelashes hid her black eyes. She peeked shyly toward Xhelal from the corner of her eyes.

Sami arrived carrying a covered dish of marinated vegetables from his mother. In ones and twos the entire staff came carrying some contribution for the feast. We loaded into the vans and headed off for Hoghoost.

As we drove through town, we passed stores selling hardware and clothing, a bakery, two small open-air coffee cafes, and an Internet café. Many businesses closed before the war; but now Gjalen was beginning to rebuild.

We waved to the American boys on the streets dressed in drab army green or jungle fatigues. They carried machine guns and stood on nearly every corner in the city. We passed a Hummer armed with machine guns, facing front and back, to guard the street in both directions. It was a common sight—the Peacekeepers—here to protect us, but it unnerved me each time we passed a convoy to see their guns aimed at us.

Young men with such serious expressions, even though I knew they were here to protect me as well as the local people, I felt a quickening in my heart whenever I met one head-on, gun pointed straight toward me, and a stern, serious expression in his eyes. It felt uneasy to depend on the judgment of an eighteen-year-old to know when, and when not, to use his gun.

The Peacekeepers were necessary—valiant referees. Sniper shootings and car bombings continued to happen in Kosovo. Only one week before, a four-year-old Serbian boy was shot, presumably accidentally, caught by the spray of a drive-by shooter. Conti, one of the drivers, returned to the office that morning and reported the shooting.

"He was just a little boy," Conti said with a dazed expression. "I think to shoot him was an accident, but I don't think he will live."

Bedreji and I sat in the office sipping strong Turkish coffee when we heard this sad news. I commented that I didn't understand why the shootings continued even now when, supposedly, the war was over.

"Oh, Nancy, you are so…what is the word for like a little girl… innocence?" Bedreji began. She went on to explain the belief in *can-nonelakadugajnit*—the code of retribution—to me.

Her people, the Muslim-Albanians, suffered most recently under a harsh orthodox Serbian government, but now the roles had reversed. Now it was the Albanians turn to avenge their families' losses.

"We are supposed to kill ten for every one of our family they took. It is the son's duty. If he fails, the duty is passed on to his son," Bedreji explained.

I asked her how she felt about the code.

"I think it is stupid," she spat. "Because of the code the fighting will never stop. My children will see war. It's stupid, and we are not a stupid people . . ." her voice trailed off in a sigh. "But, I am a modern Muslim," Bedreji said as she stood up. She looked around the room, now full of people at the end of the workday. "Not everyone here is so modern," she said softly.

Our caravan of vans left the city and headed toward Hoghoost. The pot-filled road bumped us along as we wound up into the foothills. Wild red poppies grew alongside the road and stood out against the backdrop of minty fields summer had painted; then I saw, sprawled among the poppies, winding spirals of razor wire that marked the boundaries of the Kosovo Forces base and was reminded of "The War" and of "The Code." The pleasant chatter of conversation around me became white noise behind the questions spinning about my head.

Will this small country ever reach a true peace? Will the hatred between the two ethnic groups ever stop? Will our boys—our soldiers—ever be able to go home? And if they do, will the fighting just start up again? This feuding has gone on for eons. What will it take to make real change happen?

We arrived at the large clearing with shade trees around a meadow and a good-sized stream that fell over a twelve-foot drop and created a waterfall. We unpacked the food, the tables, and chairs and spread blankets around the grass. It was a lovely picnic, complete with group showers in the waterfall, just for fun, and dancing The Valle to tinny tunes screeching out from a small portable radio. And, of course, there were several rousing games of soccer.

It was wonderful to watch the tight expressions on the young people's faces loosen and relax.

War changes people. Once lived, it is never forgotten. War's baggage was carried on these young people's shoulders. It weighed them down. It put a dullness in their step and in their eyes. At the same time, war sharpened their senses—left them hypervigilant, wary. On this day it was nice to see the group at ease, to hear their easy conversations in their own language. See them smile. Hear them laugh.

The war had ended officially only a year before. Considering their freshly wounded bodies and psyches, knowing their many losses, I was and continue today to be utterly amazed by their resilience.

I thought about how Bedreji had hinted some of the young men working with us might be ready to carry out retribution for their family's honor. The Code. I wondered if among this group of lovely young people, there were those who would actually avenge their families. I hoped not. It was hard to imagine the young men who laughed and danced and carried each other on shoulder tops into the waterfall being capable of such an act.

Perhaps, as Bedreji described, "I am innocence." But what I'd like to believe is that change can come about little by little. Perhaps this will be the generation that will make it happen. All growth comes in tiny increments. Baby steps. I can only hope. After all, the young men danced The Valle, and they did bring chips and sodas to the picnic.

MAKING THE SMALL TORTILLA

"UJRAL Q'ANWACH XOLOB."

"WE ARE THE CHILDREN OF YELLOW-FACED CORN, SPOTTED CORN."

MAYAN SAYING STILL USED TODAY

It had been hot—unbearably hot—a deep down, stinky, sticky hot that makes you breath shallow and lie still so the mosquitoes won't hear, but we were getting a reprieve from the triple-digit temperatures and almost matching humidity. A "cold-front" had blown into the steamy village and brought the oppressive heat down into the reasonable mid-seventies. My husband, Norm, and I could breathe and move again. The locals brought out their sweatshirts.

We were approaching our third month in Belize, a country still called British Honduras when I was in school. The village Punta Gorda, PG, as the locals called it, had around four thousand people. It was large enough to have a grocery store that sold everything from vegetables to tire patches, an ice cream stand/pharmacy combination, and a library that, although not cataloged or filed on shelves, did have piles and piles of old books gifted by well meaning visitors. PG had several small cafes mostly named after the proprietor. Everyone was known on a first-name basis. There was Bobby's Fish House, Grace's Chinese, and a Bed and Breakfast known simply as Chet's Place. PG had its own Water District office; however, it was pumped electrically. With intermittent electricity, sometimes we didn't have running water for days.

At the time we were there the highway that connected the village to the rest of the country was a rough, bumpy dirt road—a mud bog in the rainy season, deep with thick, red dust in the dry season. It turned into the lone paved road in town, Water Street, and ran along the edge of the turquoise Bay of Honduras.

The town was laid out in a dirt road grid from there: three streets back was our temporary clinic and six back was the little concrete house where we lived on Symphony Street.

Not nearly as attractive as the name sounds, Symphony Street was a row of unpainted wooden shanties, two to three on each side of the road. Our house was made of concrete blocks. Beyond us were two more dirt roads with similar wooden houses, and then the rainforest encroached and swallowed up the edges of the little town.

Life was slow and easy in PG, traffic minimal. Most people walked wherever they needed to go. The streets were full of barefoot children and mangy, hungry dogs that rooted through the garbage bunkers on street corners.

The homes were small and made of two distinct building materials, plain concrete blocks and rough cut lumber, usually unpainted. If the home was painted, it was in a bright fluorescent color that peeled under the hot Belizean sun. Corrugated tin was a common roof, though a few homes had grass thatch or palm fronds as was common in the smaller outlying villages.

We worked relentlessly to turn a corner of a dilapidated old building into a temporary Women's Clinic. We hauled out truck-loads of garbage, removed a termite nest the size of a Thanksgiving turkey, and scraped termite trails from the walls and ceiling. We scrubbed and mopped and painted until the clinic began at least if not to shine, to appear reasonably clean. Norm's comment was, "We wouldn't put our chickens in this back home;" however, we would have to make do for now.

Next, while I provided medical services in the makeshift space, Norm worked with the local men to build a new, permanent home for the much-needed clinic.

That's when we met Martin. Side by side, under the scorching sun, the men cleared the ever-encroaching rainforest, dug a foundation with hand tools, and poured concrete by the wheelbarrow-full. As the concrete walls were being built, a single block at a time, a special bond began to cement between Norm and his new friend Martin.

Toward the end of the clinic construction project, Martin invited us to come to his home for dinner.

"My wife, she will cook the tortilla for you," he said.

Belize is located on the isthmus of Central America with Mexico to its north and Guatemala to the south. It is an English-speaking island in a sea of Spanish. However, although English is the official language of the country, many languages and dialects are spoken. Martin's original language is Ketchi Mayan. When he began school at age five, he learned English. He now insists his children learn both languages.

We were delighted Martin was inviting us to his home and made plans for the following day. We were curious to see what Martin's wife would prepare.

Food is an important part of life. It is a reflection of the culture. Simple and pragmatic describes the Belizean approach to the cuisine we had seen so far in PG. Beans, rice, and chicken or fish made up the usual fare in cafés.

Typically in the inland villages, corn, rice, and beans complemented each other to form the primary diet protein. Occasionally, chicken was included but was usually reserved for special occasions. In a hot and humid climate with little or no refrigeration, it made sense that chicken be the meat of choice since it can be killed, plucked, cooked, and eaten in a single day, making storage not a concern.

We were awakened early the next morning by little boy voices calling, "Mr. Norm, Miss Nancy."

I crawled out of bed and padded to the window. There stood Martin's sons, Elcerio and Mariano, politely waiting outside the fence that encircled our yard, straight, black hair neatly combed, broad smiles on their sweet brown faces. They looked smart in their clean school uniforms: mint green cotton shirts and black pants. They shouted excitedly, "You are coming to dinner tonight! Me pa got a chicken for you!"

I felt humbled. Eating meat was obviously not an everyday event for them. The chicken was to honor us.

When we arrived at the home that evening, the children were all a-twitter with the excitement of having dinner guests. Their father, Martin, was outdoors, sitting by the fire, warming himself against the frigid cold front of the seventy or so degree weather that we were enjoying.

Martin's home was a wooden structure about the size of a single garage. It was made of rough-cut lumber raised off the ground on five-foot stilts to keep out the rain and the animals. It had windows, but no glass or screens to cover them, and a door opening, but no door that closed. A thick pallet of palm fronds covered the roof. Although Martin lived just at the edge of Punta Gorda, his home was built exactly like the ones in the smaller outlying villages— exactly the way they had been built for thousands of years. He was very proud, however, of the one luxury he had been able to provide for his wife—a single water spigot near the road's edge.

"Me wife, she has water to clean and to cook. She no more haul the water," he said proudly when he showed the spigot to Norm.

His wife, Cecilia, squatted in front of a small wooden table that had stubby legs, holding it about a foot off the ground. She was busy forming tortillas from the pale yellow corn mash she had ground that morning. With the ease of a woman doing a task by body memory after years and years of practice, she deftly shaped and fried the tortillas on a heavy round metal griddle over the open fire. The griddle hissed as it heated up, and a sweet odor circled our heads in musky tendrils.

Cecilia stood to meet us. She was short, only a few inches taller than ten-year-old Elcerio. Solidly built, she had a strong muscular body, the kind earned doing hard, physical work. She was barefoot and wore a faded rose-colored cotton dress in the style all the villagers wore: short puffy sleeves, princess cut bodice trimmed with frayed cotton lace, and a gathered skirt that fell below her knees.

I had seen the exact dress in a rainbow of colors—blue, green, yellow, lavender, and rose—in the villages that surrounded Punta Gorda. I suspected the color indicated a woman's original village; however, that was just my guess. Maybe they simply choose their favorite color. Cecilia smiled shyly when Martin introduced us. "I'm happy you come to our home," she said.

After introductions, I asked her if she would teach me how to make tortillas. She covered her face and giggled. "Of course, I be happy to teach you."

Cecilia grabbed a small amount of corn meal paste from a large plastic bowl and rolled it into a ball. It looked easy enough, but perhaps there was more to it than first inspection revealed. She watched my reaction out of the corner of her downcast eyes. She seemed pleased to be teaching this old white woman from so far away.

"I learned to make the tortilla from my mama. That is our way. When I was a baby, I watched her, and when I had six years, she let me begin to help. Every day for more than twenty years I have made the tortilla," Cecilia said.

Cecilia began to form a ball with the meal in her hands. "Do this," she said. I reached into the bowl, pulled out my own wad of dough, and begin to mimic her action.

Immediately, Cecilia covered her face with her forearms, since her hands were full of dough, and began to giggle.

"What? What am I doing wrong?" I asked, laughing along with her.

Blushing, Cecilia continued to giggle as she told me, "Take only a small bit, Miss Nancy. You must make the tortilla very small." She reached across my lap, pinched a small bit of dough from my ball, and threw it back in the bowl. Then she nodded her head and resumed her demonstration.

She continued to roll the dough into a ball and then patted it round and round until it formed a thin, perfectly circular patty. I attempted to mimic her by patting my tortilla round and round. Although mine came out much less than perfect, it still received praise from my teacher—praise and plenty of giggles.

We continued to form the corn meal patties until we had enough to fill the round piece of metal over the open fire she used as a stove. Each time I reached into the bowl for a wad of dough, Cecilia checked me and smiled if the amount was small enough. If I pinched off too large of a wad, she would giggle and take a pinch of it back.

As we worked, she explained the importance of making the tortilla small. "If you make the tortilla too big, then your man will know that you are lazy. All men want a woman who will make the tortilla small," Cecilia said earnestly.

I began to understand that making the tortilla was much more than simply preparing a meal. The tortilla is an indication of who a woman is. The tortilla says much more than simply "Dinner is ready."

After the tortillas were formed, Cecilia showed me how to cook them on the ungreased grill over the open fire. She showed me how to check them frequently, turning them with her bare hands so they didn't burn. When the tortillas turned a lovely beige color, with dark brown speckles, they were done. She removed them from the grill with her bare hands and placed them in a towel wrapped bowl to keep warm.

When the tortillas were ready, she shyly invited us into their home, leading the way up a ladder-like ramp into the hut. She then returned outside to fetch a large, covered, black pot and dished up bowls of stewed chicken and broth for everyone. Cecelia placed another bowl containing an orange drink in the center of the table. "We will share," she said as she set it down.

Following Martin's lead we squatted around a small table barely large enough to hold the bowls.

"Eat," said Martin. "Take your time. We have plenty."

First, we watched to see how it was done. Soon, we were dipping our tortillas into the savory stew and scooping up the delicious chunks of chicken. The stock appeared to be seasoned with cilantro and another leaf I did not recognize. Achote colored the stew a fiery red.

Giggling, Cecilia covered her face with both hands. "Wait! Wait! I forgot." She ran back outdoors and returned with tiny roasted peppers perched atop a tortilla. "It is for the chicken," she said as she demonstrated how to smear the pepper over the achote-stained meat.

Just a tiny smudge lit my mouth a-fire and I reached hastily for the bowl of orange drink in the middle of the table. The family laughed heartily at my reaction.

Such a wonderful family they were, sharing a meal and honoring us with a chicken and the small tortillas made from their sacred corn. The simplicity and abundance of their food reflected the humble, yet abundant life of Martin's family.

On an evening in the rainforest while the fan palms swayed in the cool breeze and the quiet hush of evening fell over the village, a lovely Mayan woman, Cecilia, taught me the skill of making the small tortilla. She taught me that making the tortilla is an art form and a reflection of every Mayan woman. The shape and size of her tortilla reflects the energy, the effort, and the love with which she treats the corn. Cecilia's small tortillas are also very telling of how willing she is to provide the very best possible for her family.

Corn is venerated in the Mayan culture as the very essence of life itself. The *Popol Voh*, the Mayan Bible, declares that man is made from corn. In one form or another, tortillas, mash, or the drink *pozole*, corn makes up most of the Mayan diet.

When Cecilia kneels each day beside the fire and begins to grind the limewater-soaked corn into a smooth, pasty meal, she does it with reverence. She is thankful for the corn; she is grateful to the corn. Like mothers around the world, Cecilia wants to feed and nurture her family. With corn her family will not be hungry.

In our modern world of instant gratification, where even popcorn is cooked in a microwave in a matter of minutes, I am not certain the quiet pride, nor the simple joy, this woman feels as she prepares the corn tortillas for her family can be understood.

I am not certain that I fully understand. I do know that I would like to make it my own.

THE WORLD IS A DANGEROUS PLACE

"LIFE SHRINKS OR EXPANDS IN PROPORTION TO ONE'S COURAGE."

ANAIS NIN

There's nothing like an exploding cow to get a country girl's attention. The people I worked with in Kosovo were very careful with their expatriate staff. They tried hard not to put us in danger. Sometimes the steps taken seemed to be almost careful to a fault, but "better to be safe than . . ." was their motto. You were left to fill in the blank with your imagination. Sometimes the constant undercurrent of fear made us imagine things that weren't there. Sometimes we felt they exaggerated the danger, but today's report really grabbed me.

Every morning, before we climbed into the white Land Rovers with our humanitarian organization's logo on both sides, we waited for Laura, the Office Coordinator, to return from the security meetings. She gave us a briefing before we headed out to the field to hold clinic in tiny buildings called ambulantas scattered about the Kosovo countryside. If any areas were considered "hot," which meant a recent murder or riot had occurred that day, our plans were changed.

"Okay let me have your attention," began Laura. "Near Kamanice, a grenade was thrown into a crowd of Serbian people yesterday and, in retaliation, they began stopping cars, pulling people out, and beating them. Don't go there today. Children in Partes found several live grenades. Fortunately, an adult saw them playing with the grenades and took them away before anyone was hurt. The road that leads to Pristina is blocked today. It's a protest to the increasing violence against the Serbian population. Anyone needing to go to Pristina today take the Ferizji route."

Before we loaded into the van to go out into the village, Laura reported one last item that caught my attention. "As they return to work, farmers are finding landmines in their fields. They remove them, but often simply carry them to the nearest roadside. Last week two farmers were injured when they attempted to handle mines, and yesterday, just outside of town, a heifer was blown up when she stepped on one. Several mines were reported and removed from along the road this past week. Everyone is to be particularly cognizant of this danger. There has been an increase in land mines found on the roads. Everyone be on the alert for any objects in the road. If you see any, report them to the United Nations Police. *Do not attempt to remove them yourselves!*"

With that warning echoing in our ears, we headed down the bumpy road to Novoberde to hold clinic. It was a beautiful, sunny day. The sky was filled with puffy cumulus clouds that contrasted against the deep blue sky. It was far too pretty a day for danger to be lurking out there, wasn't it?

I had been in Kosovo for a few weeks and had grown accustomed to seeing young men in uniform carrying guns on every corner and Hummers patrolling the streets. So far, there had been no reports of violence against the Peacekeepers or any of the many humanitarian workers here in the Balkans. The sniper shootings and other violence seemed to be only between the two opposing ethnic groups—Serbians and Albanians. However, an accidentally tripped landmine is a random attack. Like I said, there's nothing like an exploding cow to get my attention.

I wondered how my staff—Doctors Mirvete and Linda and nurses Bedreji and Dejetare—felt hearing the report. Each had lost at least one family member to the Balkan conflict. Each lived through a personal hell. I had heard bits and pieces of their stories, as well as other's, during the few days we spent together. An uncle's hand severed for writing against the government, a brother's unexplained disappearance, and stories of entire families fleeing their burning homes to name a few.

And while these sort of atrocities took place, these young people received their medical training in garages and basements or clandestine classes underground in the system that developed after 1981 when the Orthodox Serbian government mandated all education would be taught in the Serbian language. The Albanian-Muslims were ejected from universities as well as all government offices. They were not allowed access to the hospitals or clinics.

However, the creative, resilient Albanians responded by developing their own parallel system of government and system of taxation, education, and healthcare. It was all unofficial under the radar of the Serbian government.

Medical training was minimal to say the least; however, under the circumstances, it is incredible that they even considered studying when all around them was chaos. It took uncommon courage.

Now they were part of the rebuilding efforts in their country. Hard working and eager to learn, they were there to become better doctors. I was there to teach them.

In truth, I felt way over my head.

We were without a driver and guard that day, which was unusual. Nearly every day a male driver drove the all female medical team. In part this was for protection, but also the drivers all spoke Albanian and English. They served as interpreters if needed.

Because she had been to Novo Berde before, Rose, the German doctor and trainer who I was replacing, agreed to drive that day. In the huge Land Rover, little five-foot Rose could barely see over the steering wheel. We cracked jokes about getting her a catalog to sit on. Everyone was in high spirits. The cacophony of laughter and chatter echoed throughout the vehicle as we bumped along the terrible pot-holed road.

I had just completed my orientation at the organization's headquarters in Pristina. This was my first week in Gjalan, where I would spend the millennium summer helping these doctors and nurses practice prenatal care. I felt particularly vulnerable because I knew it was Rose's last day. The next day I would take over as medical team trainer. My head spun.

Am I up to this? Can I make a difference here? Do I know enough to teach these doctors anything? An exploding heifer…TMI…TMI…Way too much information! What the heck am I doing here?

We left town and headed out into the countryside toward the winding road that climbed into the foothills to Novo Berde. We passed cows grazing in the fields and, farther up the mountainside, sheep tended by barefoot boys who waved as we drove past. We bumped along quietly with little conversation in the van, each lost in our own thoughts.

Why did I really come to this bizarre, war-ridden county?...Am I really here to help?...Is this just a lark...an adventure, a chance to catch an adrenaline rush?...No, I've never been one for adrenaline. I like it nice and calm.

Suddenly, smack dab in the center of the right-hand lane, the very lane we were driving in, there it was—a drab green dome-shaped object about ten inches in length and half as wide. A landmine!

Those in the front seat saw it first as Rose simultaneously slammed on the brakes and screamed, "Look Out!" We careened toward the side of the road right toward the object she was trying to avoid.

The women in the backseat, thrown forward by the sudden stop, and startled by Rose's scream, cried out as well. Ten seconds of bedlam, followed by dead silence throughout the car, everyone's eyes focused on the drab green object only a few feet away from the car. We held a collective breath.

Private thoughts ricocheted about my head. I am certain each of the women had their own stream of consciousness flowing too. Every one of them had lost at least one family member during the war. Each had lived the horror, up close and personal. They had seen firsthand what damage a landmine could do. They might have been having flashbacks of other landmines. I could only imagine. I questioned why I was there, in a foreign country—one where landmines were found on country roads! *I'm a grandmother! What am I thinking?*

Then, ever so slowly, little protrusions extended from the mine—two along the longer sides and a single extension on one of the shorter sides.

At the exact same moment, we all realized what the landmine actually was. A riot of laughter broke out among us as that old turtle began to finish his slow trip across the road.

We proceeded down the bumpy, pot-hole-filled road to Novo Berde, laughing hysterically.

One of my favorite sayings, about how "the lowly turtle only makes progress when she sticks her neck out" came to mind. I tried to tell it to the others, but something got lost in the translation. They didn't understand, though it made perfect sense to me.

Coming to Kosovo was a stretch—way out of my comfort zone—removed from the technologies of modern medicine. I didn't know if I could make a difference in this shambled country. I didn't know if I was up to the task. However, it is only when we extend ourselves, when we take real risks, that true growth can take place.

The country was Kosovo—a country with much work to be done—so much it was overwhelming. A medical team of lovely Kosovar women struggling to rebuild their lives and their country bumped down a pot-filled road toward Nove Berde together. Each lived through horrible times, witnessed terrible things, and suffered large losses, yet they were able to study long hours, show up for work every day, and find humor in "a mine that grew legs." It was a van full of strong, beautiful women, every single one with their neck stretched out—way out.

In God's Palm

"Courage doesn't always roar. Sometimes it is
that quiet voice at the end of the day saying
tomorrow I will begin again."

Anonymous

"Why'd you go and take your baby off the titty?" Felicita
demanded in a loud lyrical voice. A dark scowl wrinkled her broad,
black forehead. "Now why'd ya go and do that?"

Felicita, nurse for the surrounding villages, towered before the
group of tiny Mayan women who stood in the middle of the road.
An immense woman in both height and girth, her blue striped seer-
sucker uniform suggested a military milieu. With both hands on her
broad hips, she looked vexed and frustrated and was such a formidable presence that I, along with every other woman in the group,
knew we were all in serious trouble.

Felicita allowed me, a North American nurse, to observe her
immunization clinics in the villages that day. She was the Public
Health Nurse for Columbia Village and the dozen or so smaller
villages in a twenty-mile radius of her clinic. Columbia Village
is in southern Belize, about fifteen miles north of the Guatemala
border.

Felicita's clinic was a dank, unpainted concrete block building in
the center of Columbia Village. On the days when she wasn't traveling to the smaller surrounding village to do outreach and immunizations, her clinic was open for whatever medical emergency might
appear. She treated everything from the exotic snakebite to the
mundane bloody nose. She lived in a small apartment above her

clinic and was on-call twenty-four hours a day. This is the norm for all rural nurses in Belize.

Nursing requires four years of university in Belize, the equivalent of a baccalaureate degree in the States. The training is intense and arduous; as well it must be since the rural Public Health Nurse must function essentially as a complete healthcare system for her entire area. Felicita wasn't simply the village nurse. The scope of her practice was awesome. She was the nurse, doctor, social worker, midwife, and ambulance service for her villages.

As we entered each village, Eltario, Felicita's driver, blasted the truck horn to alert the mothers we were coming. We stopped in the middle of the dusty road, climbed out of the truck, and lowered the tailgate to serve as an exam table. Candeleria, Felicita's assistant, climbed up in the back of the truck and slid two cardboard boxes forward to our reach. The village clinic was ready.

Within minutes women dressed in a rainbow of bright traditional dress emerged from their thatched roof huts. Toddlers and children trailed behind. They carried their babies in white cotton slings across their backs, a supporting band across their foreheads.

They each seemed to know their own part in the choreography of a village clinic. Felicita queried each mother about her own health, her baby's health, and then the rest of the family. At the same time she drew up the immunizations.

One at a time the shy, gentle, browned-skinned women handed their baby-filled slings to me. Using the same block-and-tackle equipment by fisherman to weigh fish, I held the apparatus up high and read aloud each baby's weight for Candeleria to record. Eltario wandered off to afford the women privacy.

Most of the mothers brought an empty jar or can for the liquid Acetaminophen Felicita poured from a gallon jar. New mothers and any others who forgot were sent scampering back to their grass-thatched hut in search of a container for the cherry-red elixir.

"If the baby feels hot or is fussy, give him one spoonful in the morning and one at lunch and one in the evening," she told them. "If he feels hot in the night, give him one spoonful."

I wondered whether they even had spoons in their primitive little huts and, if so, what size? But the system here seemed to be working, so my questions were merely passing thoughts, flitting through my head like rainforest butterflies without real need for an answer.

A worn looking young woman stepped forward with her baby. Her tired face and the dullness in her dark eyes spoke volumes. I saw the weariness from struggling hard to live off the land, a deep-drained tired that ran clear to her core.

She handed me her baby-filled sling and softly announced, "Emitario." The sling was feather light. *This must be a newborn*, I thought. Then Candeleria pulled his card from the cardboard file and announced his birth date. Little Em was four months old!

Holding the block and tackle high above my head, I looped his sling on the hook. A chill passed through me as I read out loud— about eight pounds—not nearly enough for a four-month-old baby.

Felicita's broad brow wrinkled into a skeptical frown. She stepped closer, reread the scale, peered inside the baby-filled hammock, then turned toward the mother. She put both hands on her broad hips and asked bluntly, "Do you give your baby the titty?"

Looking away, the mother mumbled, "No, not anymore."

The tirade began. "Why'd ya take your baby off the titty? Now why'd ya go and do that?" Felicita thundered. "Don't you know there's nothing in the world better for him?"

"He stopped. He was sick almost a month ago with the diarrhea and he won't suck now," the young mother mumbled, looking at the ground.

Felicita came alive. Concern flashed in her dark eyes. "Does he still have diarrhea?" she asked, taking tiny Emitario, sling and all, from me.

"No, not now," the young mother replied defensively, sensing Felicita's disapproval. "He did for one week. He will suck the bottle, so I put honey in it for him to get him strong,"

Sitting on the tailgate of the truck, Felicita slowly removed tiny Emitario from his hammock and gently undressed him. Dry, loose skin hung on his frail, bird-like bones. His eyes were sunken and lacked the shine and sparkle of a healthy baby. They held only dull acceptance. He did not cry as she examined him, nor did he struggle away from her. It was as if this baby boy accepted he was no longer of this world.

Felicita barked orders to me to dig into a cardboard box and find the electrolyte solution mix. I rummaged deep but found only two packets, enough for two quarts. The baby was both dehydrated and malnourished. An ominous shadow passed over. I didn't know the statistics specifically for Belize, but I did know conservative estimates for all Third World countries say that every minute eight babies die—mostly from infection, malnutrition, or diarrhea. *Two quarts will not make much difference*, I thought to myself.

"You must mix this powder with water and give to Em every hour until it is gone. Do you have sugar and salt in your home?" Felicita demanded.

"Yes," the woman whispered looking at the ground.

Still, in a no-nonsense manner, she instructed the young mother to boil water and mix six spoons of sugar and four pinches of salt in the water. "Give it to him every hour until I come back. We must get special milk for Em until he learns to nurse again. For now, you tell your man he must get canned milk for your baby. Emitario is very, very sick. You must teach little Em how to suck again." In an encouraging voice, she continued, "With only a few weeks since he stopped, it may be possible."

Then, loudly, for the benefit of all the women gathered in the middle of the road, Felicita announced, "There is nothing in the world better for your babies than the milk from your titty. If the baby stops sucking, he will not grow. He will become sick. Honey is not good for your baby. It can make him sick. Titty is good for your baby. It will make your baby strong and thick."

I admired how she turned this tragedy into a learning experience for all the village women and felt a swell of respect for this pragmatic, plain-speaking nurse.

We completed the weights, exams, and immunizations and headed down the road where we repeated the same process again and again in village after village until the day was spent. I, too, was spent. I felt bone-tired, weary and so, so wretched. In three days Felicita would return to the village to assess little Emitario, but she told me that she wasn't optimistic.

"He is so little. She is so tired," she said.

We drove down the bumpy, dusty road in silence, reversing the early morning route that brought us to the isolated villages. I offered to buy the formula for little Em, but Felicita looked sadly out of the truck window toward the horizon as she replied, "And can you buy the milk next week and next month and the next and the next and the next? No, buying milk will not help this baby or the other village babies." She turned toward me. Her sad but steady gaze met mine. Then, with a slight shrug, she looked away and softly sighed. "He's already in God's palm."

Such a challenging job. Such a formidable presence. Felicita is fearless. She plunges into her work every day and encourages women to take charge of their lives. She supports and applauds them to do their very best. Then, recognizing what she can't change, accepts it all unconditionally. And everyday when the sun drops below the towering rainforest trees in the calm surrender of evening, Felicita knows that tomorrow she will begin again.

SECTION THREE

WHEREVER THERE IS GREAT LOVE

OVER COFFEE WITH SISTER FILJE

"WHEREVER THERE IS GREAT LOVE, THERE ARE ALWAYS MIRACLES."

WILLA CATHER

*N*othing happens in Kosovo before coffee, or more aptly put, everything happens over coffee. I spent the summer of 2000 working in the war recovery effort in Kosovo. A nurse practitioner, I trained local nurses and doctors to provide prenatal care in remote villages six days a week. On Sundays we rested.

One Sunday, my friend and driver, Salami offered to take me to mass in a nearby village. That's how I met Sister Filje, in the mountain village of Latnice in the former Yugoslavia, an old county with many new names—Bosnia, Herzegovina, Croatia, Macedonia, Montenegro, Serbia, and Kosovo—located due east of Rome, Italy, across the Adriatic Sea, and inland from Montenegro and Albania.

Sister Filje, a feisty little Albanian nun, is also a nurse. In fact, she was the entire healthcare system for her village.

Red tiled roofs of the villagers' homes dotted the mountainside. In the valley below stood a simple, yet beautiful, four-hundred-year-old church with a tall, stark, steeple that soared toward the sky. Next to the church was a small, plainly furnished clinic.

Sister Filje was waiting for us when we drove up the winding dirt road to the clinic. Salami had sent a message to her through a friend earlier in the week that we would visit before mass. She answered our knock at the door and greeted us with a wide smile and a firm handshake.

"*Miremengjes*," she said. "Good morning."

Sister Filje was probably no more than thirty-five years old. Slightly built, her black traditional nun's dress almost seemed to swallow her up, and her dark brown hair peeked out from under her habit. Her kind brown eyes were luminous and expressive, and a dimple in her right cheek appeared and disappeared as she spoke.

She proudly invited us into her clinic, and proud she had reason to be. Unlike the filthy government-run *ambulantas* I had been working in, where we might have to run a rodent out in the morning, or at the very least clean up their droppings from the floor, Sister Filje's clinic was spotless. Sparkling glass containers holding small amounts of gauze, cotton balls, and tongue depressors lined the countertops. The exam table, a worn leather-covered cot, was draped in a lovely, pristine-white crocheted tablecloth. A tiny embroidered pillow lay on it, ready to cradle her next patient's head.

Sister Filje spoke only Albanian. I speak only English. After introducing us to each other, Salami translated that she was inviting us for coffee. This is a significant custom, and no matter where you are, in a home, a school, or a hospital, you are offered Turkish coffee. It is the polite thing to do. It is also the polite thing to accept. To decline is unthinkable.

Soon we were balancing miniature cups on child-size saucers and stirring them with tiny spoons. As I sipped the thick, black sludge, flashbacks of childhood tea parties involving mud tea danced through my head. As is common among nurses, we talked about our work. I asked Sister Filje to describe a typical day in her clinic.

"Yesterday," she replied, "I treated all six of the Rexhepi children for chicken pox. Then I cleaned the earwax from an old man's ears so he could hear just a little of today's mass. Later in the afternoon I sewed a long cut in a young man's leg; he'd gashed it with a sharp hand tool. I see many such cuts now that the tractors are gone. Our men work only with hand tools now." Her comment about the tractors reminded me how hard life is for the Kosovo farmers since all farm equipment was confiscated by the military during the war.

Sister Filje told us her work involved not only providing medical care for her patients but also providing social services in the village. Sometimes that meant cooking soup and delivering it to patients who were ill. Sometimes, when the day-to-day stresses of living began to fray at the fabric of a family, she was there to offer counseling. Sometimes she got to distribute clothing donated by an American church to the village's children.

"Now, that is a fun thing to do." She winked.

The Catholic Church had stationed her in the village fourteen years ago. Her tenure spanned both before and during the recent Balkan War. Latnice had been less affected by the decade-long political unrest than most villages in Kosovo. The conflict was between Orthodox Serbians, who were in power, and the Muslim-Albanians. Latnice was an oddity in Kosovo. The entire village was Croatian and Catholic. For the most part, both sides spared the village.

Sister Filje's job wasn't easy though, as she dealt with plenty of suffering every day. However, despite the misery she saw, she had a resiliency that belied her petite size and quiet demeanor. She maintained a positive attitude and a delightful sense of humor.

Sister provided complete holistic care for her village with one exception. She didn't like to deliver babies. She preferred to transport her laboring patients to the nearest "health house"—the rough equivalent to a small rural hospital in the States. If she could prevent it, Sister Filje didn't deliver babies in her clinic.

As we sipped the cups of pungent coffee sludge, Salami and I saw Sister Filje glow as she described her days. It was obvious this was much more than simply her job. It was her mission. Her work was love.

I asked her to tell me some of her most interesting nursing experiences in Latnice. Bear in mind that my translator, Salami, speaks Albanian very well but speaks only a little English. I am certain much was lost in the translations, but as I understood it, this is what Sister Filje told us . . .

"A young woman came to the clinic late one night in labor. I was familiar with this patient. I knew she was pregnant, and I knew the woman was not normal," Sister said.

Whether she meant that the woman was mentally ill or developmentally delayed was unclear. Perhaps she meant that the pregnancy had not progressed normally. The details were vague, but this much I did understand, the woman was in active labor, and for Sister Filje, "Delivering babies, gives me too much fright!"

So, even though Sister had already dressed for bed, she quickly loaded the woman into her little, beat-up, beige Yugo and sped off into the night, bumping down the rut-filled road with the laboring woman screaming loudly in both fear and pain.

"I was terrified. I prayed hard for the baby not to come," Sister Filje said as she relived the story for us. "She screamed so loud. I thought to myself, *The health house is too far away. I will drive to the soldiers' base and the doctors there will help us because this is an emergency*, but they said, 'No. Drive on to Viti to the health house. This woman is Albanian. We can only serve Serbians. The doctor in Viti will deliver her baby.'"

Frustrated and frightened, Sister Filje sped off again into the night, completely convinced the baby would come before they reached the health house. As she told the story, she patted her chest quickly in pantomime of her racing heartbeat, and her eyes were wide with fright. Yet, the mischief still danced in her dark brown eyes, and the dimple in her left check winked at me.

They did arrive in Viti before the baby was born, and she was delivered safely, mere minutes after they arrived. The infant girl was named Christian in honor of the nun. It was only after mother and newborn were settled into bed for the night that Sister Filje realized she was standing in the health house clad only in her pajamas. She blushed with embarrassment and quickly departed, retracing her path home along the dark bumpy road.

In all the excitement, she had completely forgotten that a nine o'clock curfew had been set by the government and was being firmly enforced by the Peacekeeping Forces. Violators were being incarcerated.

At the military checkpoint she was stopped and made to get out of her car by two machine gun-toting young men dressed in drab army green. They inspected her car and interrogated the little nun. She was mortified as she stood before the guards in the bright beam of their flashlights wearing only her thin blue pajamas. Blushing bright red, she tried to explain why she was out so late in the night and why she wasn't properly dressed.

"I do not know what they thought of me. Perhaps they wondered what kind of woman works so late in the night wearing only her pajamas, eh?" she joked. "And I think they did not believe that

I am 'Sister' Filje," she said with a wink and, once again, that sweet dimple. She pantomimed being handcuffed by crossing her wrists.

"They arrested you?" I asked incredulously.

Sister Filje laughed. "Yo, yo, yo," she said.

Even I could translate that meant, "No, no, no."

We all shared a hearty laugh over the image of the little nun standing outdoors in her pajamas trying to convince the soldiers what had just happened.

I asked her to tell me about the most complicated patient she had ever treated.

"In my ambulanta, God made a miracle," she said solemnly. She went on to explain that an elderly woman had come to her with a huge lump in her breast. Sister Filje tried to get help from the nearby military base's medical facility. Solders from several countries were stationed in Kosovo as Peacekeepers, and these allied forces maintained a modern clinic and a small hospital near Sister Filje's village. The soldiers, however, turned the nun and the old woman away at the gate. They told Sister Filje to take the woman to the large government hospital in Pristina, more than three hours away by car.

The hospital in Pristina would certainly have treated the woman, had Sister Filje been able to get her there. But convincing her to ride in a car for the short, ten-minute drive from the village to the military base had been difficult enough. Until that day, the elderly woman had never left her village or even ridden in a car. The idea of traveling to the city was simply more than she could handle. She adamantly refused.

"Take me home," she told the nun. "I want to die in my village,"

"What was I to do?" Sister Filje asked with a mischievous smile lighting her face and making that dimple wink again. "So, we returned to my *ambulanta*, and I did the surgery myself. No anesthesia! I cut out the cancer, and then I gave her all the antibiotics on my shelf. Now, thank you, God, she is well. No infection. No carcinoma. God did a miracle in my clinic!"

Our cups were empty, save for the fine ground sediment that remained in the bottom, and it was time for us to go. The morning had flown by, and I wished for more time with Sister Filje, more time to hear stories over miniature cups of thick, dark coffee.

A few days later I left Kosovo and returned to my Midwestern home. Once there, I told this story to many of my colleagues in the medical field. Most responded with an incredulous, "Humph, it was probably just an abscess," or a more sympathetic, "Benign breast lump, maybe?"

Certainly, as professionals in one of the most technologically advanced medical systems in the world, their skepticism is understandable. I might have been just as unconvinced as my colleagues before I met the remarkable nun with luminous brown eyes and a dimple in her cheek that winked as she told her stories.

Sister Filje touched me with her down-to-earth approach to a difficult job; her work made lighter by a healthy dose of humor daily. Sister's feet are pragmatically planted on terra firma, but she is not of this world. She is a conduit through which pure Love flows.

Everything becomes known over coffee in Kosovo, and this much I know for sure: Everyday in Sister Filje's clinic, gashes will be stitched, ringworm will be treated; broken arms will be splinted, ear-wax will be removed from old men's ears, and miracles will happen.

LILLIAN'S LIFE

"WHERE THERE IS LOVE, THERE IS LIGHT."

MAHATMA GANDI

It has been years since fortune's smile blessed me with the gift of Lillian, but I can see her clearly in my mind's eye. A stooped old woman shuffles down the walk weatherworn by time and circumstance. Her light blue maid's uniform hangs loosely on her stooped and shapeless body. In one hand she carries a pink plastic pail filled with cleaning supplies and salve for a blistered tourist. Swollen legs protrude below her loose skirt revealing skin cracked like the bark on a gumbo-limbo tree. Ulcerated ankles ooze clear pale-yellow fluid. Each step a painful effort, as if walking across a beach of broken shells. She stops and raises her map-lined face from its stooped, humped-over position. Warm deep-well amber eyes crinkle as she smiles a tooth-gapped smile, then shuffles on down the walk, chuckling as she disappears behind a red hibiscus bush.

A dark-skinned man with a scruffy beard wearing a brightly flowered red shirt stood in the middle of the small airport waving a hand-printed sign with our name on it. He grabbed up our bags and hurried outside, but before we could even climb into his van he popped off the tops of a couple of Red Stripe beers for us and introduced himself as Nigel.

"Welcome to my Jamaica."

Inwardly I groaned. My brain already felt fuzzy. I didn't need to add alcohol to the mix. *I'm tired*, my inner voice whined. *Deep down tired—"my muscles lie on tired bones"—tired...just want to go lie in the sun and not talk to anyone.*

"People come from all over the world to my Jamaica. They come to drink deep of three things—my warm Jamaica sun, my Jamaica Rum, and my Red Stripe Beer," Nigel said in a velvet voice as he handed us each a bottle and popped the lid off another for himself. "Drink deep," he smiled.

Let me at that sun of his, I thought as I clinked my bottle against the men's in a toast. I was in Jamaica to recharge my drained batteries. I'd just completed a rigorous program of training as a Nurse Practitioner at the University of Southwest Texas in Dallas. An alternative training program in Women's Health, it crammed two years of didactic study into five short months, then sent us back to our communities to complete preceptorships. I felt exhausted. My cup was empty.

As my husband, Norm, had bluntly put it when he told me about this vacation—"You don't look so good." He was right. I didn't look so good, and I felt like I looked. Old. Worn. Tired.

But he had the answer. We were going to Jamaica! I could lie on the beach and let the sun recharge me or recline on a chaise by the pool and sip fancy drinks from coconuts with pineapple spears and little colored umbrellas sticking out the top. "All you need is a vacation," he said.

What I wanted to say was that what I truly needed was a couple of weeks on the couch, curled up under a quilt eating junk food and reading mysteries and trashy novels—mind-candy. I needed to recharge my body and my mind by being idle for a bit; but who can say no to paradise? Besides, the tickets were already purchased.

Before I could turn around, we were in Montego Bay, drinking Red Stripe beer while Nigel loaded our bags into his van. Then we were sped off in the direction of the resort.

As Nigel drove down the narrow paved road, I watched the slide show through my backseat window. Jamaica, a beautiful tropical country with swaying palms, lush undergrowth, and bright blue sky looked just like the pictures in a travel magazine.

What the magazines don't show, however, are the galvanized tin makeshift shacks that line the roads, where sad-eyed, thin, brown-skinned children play among even thinner pigs that root for garbage, and mangy chickens peck about grassless yards.

The advertisements don't show the pubescent young women

wearing short, tight skirts that would barely cover their panties, if they had been wearing panties—"working girls." And I mean girls in the most literal sense. Some of these young women offering themselves up to any tourist for less than the price of a six-pack of Red Stripe were barely into their teens.

Life in Jamaica appeared to be vivid, visceral, and sad, scarred by the wounds of poverty and powerlessness. But travel posters don't show this reality, only endless white sand beaches and sun-lit turquoise water.

We arrived at the resort. A tall wrought-iron gate towered in front of us across the road. Nigel stopped at the guardhouse beside the gate and hailed a sleepy-eyed boy dressed in a khaki uniform sitting inside.

"Jeffrey, be quick, mon, open the gate," he barked.

Jeffrey slowly rose from his perch on a stool inside the guardhouse and lumbered lankily to the gate, dragging it open. We drove through, and as he closed the gate behind us, I felt we had entered another Jamaica—the Jamaica of the travel posters. The real country was locked outside. The idea was so depressing that I didn't allow it to re-enter my mind for several days. It wasn't until I met Lillian that I allowed myself to reflect again on life in the real Jamaica.

Lillian was the maid who kept our room sparkling. Her attention to detail was amazing, from the fancy fan-folded toilet paper to the single fresh purple flower she left daily on the table. Clean crisp sheets and starched pillowcases appeared magically while we were out of the room.

I was amazed how quickly she worked. Her appearance didn't lend itself to that expectation. Lillian moved about the resort in a slow shuffle as if walking was painful. She had light brown weathered skin. Years of living under the sun only eighteen degrees north of the equator had thickened and dried her face into a roadmap of creases. She stooped forward, bent from a rounded hump between her shoulders. The nurse in me named it kyphosis, but my poet knew that Lillian was bent by time and circumstance.

Too self-absorbed in my own pity-party, the first few days I barely acknowledged her and responded to her cheerful, "Good morning, Miss," with only a nod and moved on. I only wanted to lie in the sun and let it bake me well.

By the third day I began to feel rested. You would think that my attitude would have improved as well, but now I had horrendous sunburn to lament. Rather than let the sun bake me well again, I had succeeded in becoming "well-baked"…to a bright red-blistered degree!

I parked myself on a bench in the shade near our room and planned to spend the day reading. As I sat there, I saw Lillian limping up the walk toward our room. As she approached, I noticed, for the first time, her swollen feet, edematous with fluids, skin cracked where her arches ought to be, oozing ulcers at her ankles. *Congestive Heart Failure*, my nurse-voice diagnosed, reminded of several of my patients with the same condition. *Feet not willing to carry where her heart can no longer go*, sang my poet.

As Lillian passed the bench and greeted me, as usual, with her warm, "Good morning, Miss," I responded. "Good day to you too. My name is Nancy. I want to thank you for taking such good care of us. Our room is lovely, thanks to you." The road map of Lillian's face shifted; her lips parted in a broad smile revealing several gaps where teeth were missing.

"It is my pleasure, ma'am, and my name is Lillian. How are you on this fine day?" she asked with a twinkle in her eyes. "Looks like m'lady has had too much Jamaica sun."

I laughed in agreement and nodded. Meeting this old women's gaze, I noticed her kind, amber-colored eyes. I was filled with a profound sense of peace that seemed to emote from this tired old women's body. I felt a stirring—a sense of connection—as though I could almost feel her gentle spirit reaching out to soothe my sunburnt arms. Lillian shuffled on down the walk, and I returned to my book, slightly unnerved by the power of our brief exchange.

The following day as I sat restless on my bench lamenting to myself how, sentenced to the shade, I was missing all the fun, Norm had gone snorkeling. Lillian came hobbling slowly down the path carrying a pink plastic bucket filled with cleaning supplies.

"Good day, Miss Nancy."

"Good day, Miss Lillian," I replied. "And how is your day today?"

"Oh, Miss Nancy, it is a very good day." She stopped. Smiling, she bent over to rummage through her plastic bucket and retrieved a small jar containing a pale yellow jelly-like substance. Its worn label read, "Island Spice Jerk Seasoning," obviously not the present contents of the jar.

"It's a very good day when I can help a friend. Use this on your burn, Miss. It will heal you."

Handing me the jar, she picked up her bucket and shuffled on down the walk. My surprised, "Thanks," followed her as she disappeared around a huge hibiscus bush.

What is it, I wondered? I opened the jar and looked at the sticky ooze inside. It resembled something like an equal mixture of honey and Elmer's Glue. I brought the jar to my nose. Yuck! The acrid, bitter smell pierced my senses—Ode de Island this stuff was not! Replacing the lid, I sat the jar beside me on the bench and resumed reading.

I was distracted. Lillian kept entering my thoughts. I wondered about her. What was her story? I marveled at what appeared, to me, to be a pretty rotten day of cleaning up after tourists and living inside a body that was obviously worn out, how Lillian could still describe the day as "a very good day" just because she thought she could help me. I eyed the jar sitting beside me.

What the heck, I thought, *the least I can do is try the stuff*.

I returned to my room, showered, and gently sponged off the lotion I slathered on that morning in an attempt to soothe my braised skin. I patted myself dry and applied the stinky, sticky ooze to my entire body—from the skin stretched across my forehead to my tender toes.

When Norm returned, his greeting words were, "Great snorkeling! Sorry you had to miss it…*what* is that smell?"

"Lillian's voodoo salve," I replied mysteriously. "It's supposed to cure what ails me."

Norm mumbled a suggestion that I might want to shower before dinner, but I just smiled. Over the afternoon the fire across my shoulders had gone out and my face no longer felt like a piece of leather stretched tight across a drum. Maybe Lillian's salve was working.

The next morning I woke up to a beautiful golden tan—something my fair skin had never experienced before. I couldn't wait to show Lillian and was disappointed when a different maid came carrying the pink plastic bucket of cleaning supplies—a young woman with rich cocoa-colored skin and thick, curly hair drawn up in a high ponytail.

"Good day, Miss," I said. "Won't Lillian be coming today?"

She told me it was Lillian's time off and that she probably had gone to visit her daughter on the other side of the island. She would be back day after tomorrow.

I spent the next two days being a tourist—playing in the water and the sun, swimming, snorkeling, and dancing late into the night under a diorama of stars. But the entire time Lillian was in the back of my mind. I was curious about the old woman—this wellspring of wisdom and warmth, who seemed so comfortable in her well-worn body and content with her life—both which, from my perspective, seemed sorely lacking. Such a strong woman. What was the source of her strength?

When she returned to work the following day, I greeted her brightly, "Good day, Miss Lillian. Did you enjoy your time off?" and was rewarded with a rich toothless smile, crinkles formed around her well-deep, kind amber eyes.

"Oh, yes, Miss. Thank you. Indeed I did, and now aren't you looking pretty with your Jamaica tan!"

I laughed and thanked her repeatedly for the salve. "What is in it anyway?" I questioned. "The stuff is magical!"

"Oh, Miss, I can't be telling you about the magic now." Lillian picked up her pink plastic pail and shuffled down the walk, chuckling as she went.

During the remaining days of my Jamaican holiday, Lillian and I continued to greet each other daily and have short, but meaningful, conversations. I learned she had three children—two sons and a daughter. The older son had moved to Canada and occasionally sent money home to his mother. The younger had "let the demon ganja take control of his spirit," and she seldom saw him even though he lived just on the other side of the island. A devout Christian, she prayed for him daily.

"I just give my troubles to the Lord and He takes care of them by and by," she said.

Her daughter lived a two-hour bus ride away with her common-law husband. They had four children whom she adored. She visited them every week on her days off from work.

"Those four babies are the angels in my life," Lillian said.

I tried not to show my surprise when I learned she was only five years older than me. Life had not been kind to Lillian. It took its toil on her body, but her spirit showed no scars from the pummeling. Ever optimistic, ever content, she impressed me daily with her hopeful attitude and easy smile.

I learned that her husband had "taken a walk away" when she was expecting her third baby. Her daughter never knew her father. Lillian raised her three children with the help of her mother, now "passed over." She worked in the sugarcane fields as a younger woman and was thrilled when she was given a job as maid at this resort ten years ago. "I am very lucky to have such easy work," she said.

Daily, my appreciation for this woman grew. Ever restless, ever seeking myself, I wondered how she could be so contented, so accepting. One day I asked her how she stayed so upbeat.

"Oh, Miss, I just count my blessings and give all my troubles to the Lord," she answered.

Departure day arrived. Our plane left at noon. We would leave the resort soon. Norm had gone to the office to check out. I sat waiting on my bench for Lillian. I wanted to say good-bye.

I saw her coming down the walkway, bent over, shuffling slowly as if walking barefoot over seashells. I had thought to myself earlier about how Lillian walked with God, but I decided then that it is God who walks with Lillian. They shuffle about the island of Jamaica together and spread joy.

Lillian's magic isn't found only in her lotions and potions. It is in her contagious, miraculous ability to bring a shift in the minds of people, from the common, "What can I get?" to her remarkable, "What can I give?" slant of thinking.

And Lillian's power lies in her absolute faith. When she surrenders her problems, no matter how large, to her Higher Power, she knows in her bones an answer will come. Lillian never questions the answer.

As she neared my bench, an American couple approached her from the opposite direction. She stopped, set down her pink pail, and mopped her face with a large wrinkled bandana pulled from her hip pocket. I heard her say, "Well, good day to you, Miss Sally, and to you, Meester John. So you've come again to my beautiful Jamaica, have you? Welcome."

I couldn't help overhearing their conversation. I gathered that this couple had been here often—returning again and again to this lovely Jamaica inside the resort gates. I was impressed that Lillian remembered their names. She must meet hundreds of visitors coming and going every week—clean all their rooms, scrub scores of toilets, fold the hundreds of rolls of toilet paper into tiny, perfect fans, place hundreds of single purple flowers in vases on the tables, and greet hundreds with a bright, "Good day."

The man asked Lillian how she had been since their last visit. She raised her head from its stooped position. Although his shoulder blocked my view, I knew she was looking at him straight in the eyes with her signature, well-deep amber gaze as she replied softly,

"Oh, I have been very good. I am blessed. I have life, and life is enough."

PLEASE HELP MY SON NOT DIE

"THERE IS NO MISTAKING LOVE. YOU FEEL IT IN YOUR
HEART. IT IS THE COMMON FIBER OF LIFE, THE FLAME
THAT LIGHTS OUR SOUL, ENERGIZES OUR SPIRIT AND
SUPPLIES PASSION TO OUR LIVES. IT IS OUR CONNECTION
TO GOD AND TO EACH OTHER."

ELIZABETH KUBLER-ROSS

My first day in the field in Kosovo was June 6, 2000. I had been in the country for two weeks. My luggage, lost in transit, arrived the day before. I saw it as a good sign.

However, over the next three months I found myself spiraling down into the abyss we call Evil. I saw and heard of things I had never before even imagined. Thankfully, I was also uplifted to extraordinary heights when I witnessed the kindness, compassion, and love that mark the other end of the continuum of human behavior. I came to realize that Evil is not an abstract thought, but a very real force in the world. More importantly, I confirmed the power of Love.

The medical project was part of a larger mission to implement modern healthcare in the Balkans as part of the war recovery effort. Working with an international humanitarian organization, my job was to train Kosovar doctors and nurses to provide prenatal care. And since the notion of seeing a healthcare provider throughout her pregnancy was foreign to the village women, we also had to sell the idea too through community education and one-on-one interactions.

At first, I felt uncomfortable with the idea that I, a nurse practitioner from the States, was to teach Kosovar doctors; however, once the history was explained, it made perfect sense. Medical training for the Albanian-Kosovor doctors had been thwarted by the political unrest over the years, and they were forced to develop a separate, parallel system of medical education from their Serbian counterparts. Their training was sorely lacking. My job was to help fill in the gaps of their knowledge base and provide guidance through didactic studies in the office and on-the-job supervised experience in the *ambulantas*—small, sparsely furnished clinics—scattered around the countryside.

I was their leader, but everyday, in so many ways, I learned so much more than I taught. Even my very first day as their trainer I relearned an important, but long-forgotten lesson: Miracles happen. Miracles happen naturally wherever there is love.

We began as a team of five women—two doctors, Linda and Mirvete, and two nurses, Bedreji and Dejetare, all from Kosovo—and me. We loaded the van with all the supplies needed to take to the village Sllatina. There we would hold a clinic for women where we provide education, exams, and medications. We would refer serious problems to the nearest health house, the equivalent to a small hospital, and provide transportation if needed. We would also provide community education to the small groups of people who clustered about the *ambulanta* to see what was happening. Education would be the most important thing we would bring to the villages.

In Kosovo, women and babies balanced precariously on the brink between life and death. Kosovo is part of Europe, but not the modern Europe of travel posters. Healthcare in Kosovo, particularly in the villages, operated like several hundreds of years ago. Women weren't seen by a healthcare provider throughout their pregnancy, nor were they educated in the warnings signs of a problem in the pregnancy—signs that indicate the mother, or her baby's, life might be in danger.

Because many of the villagers couldn't read or write, we prepared a booklet with pictures depicting the dangers—bleeding, swelling of feet or face, headache and blurry vision, lack of fetal movement, gush of water, persistent backache, or contractions before thirty-seven weeks—to reinforce what we taught.

Neonatal tetanus, virtually an unknown problem in the developed world, was a common cause of newborn death in Kosovo. By simply providing the mother with two doses of vaccine during her pregnancy, that problem would be eliminated.

We packed the van with everything we needed to hold a clinic. One large trunk contained medicines and vitamins, another basic medical equipment and supplies. Five-gallon jerry cans held the water we would need for hand washing.

The *ambulantas* were just rough small buildings. Some had electricity; others didn't. A few had running water, most didn't. Usually they had three small rooms. We used one for a waiting room; the others served as exam rooms. If there was a bathroom, it consisted of a closet-size room with a hole in the floor for squatting over.

Just as we finished loading the van, an old woman, dressed in a simple, navy-blue, cotton dress and sensible shoes, arrived. She had a large port-wine birthmark that covered the entire left side of her face and the right side of her mouth drooped flaccidly, causing spittle to collect in the corner when she talked. I suspected that she had experienced a stroke sometime in the past. I estimated that she was in her mid sixties but learned later that Doctor Drita was much younger. Hard times and horror had taken their toll, turned her hair to gray, and left deep creases of worry on her already disfigured face. But when I looked into her eyes, I saw only kindness and the twinkle of humor that I would learn was her hallmark.

The old women spoke to Doctor Linda in Albanian. From Linda's expression, it seemed she delivered an upsetting message.

"What is it?" I asked.

"She is Doctor Drita. She says she is part of us. She says she is to work with our team. But she is a pediatrician. We are women's care. I think it is a mistake," Linda said.

Puzzled, I extended my hand to the old woman and introduced myself. "Hello, I'm Nancy."

"*Une'jam* Drita," she responded with a warm smile, eyes crinkling at the corners.

I excused myself from the group and went inside the office to try to call the main office to determine if, indeed, Doctor Drita was part of my staff.

Often communications were a challenge in Kosovo. This morning the telephone in the office was dead, which was not unusual. It was unusual, however, that the short-wave radio wasn't able to squeak and squawk out a brief static-filled message to headquarters. Frustrated, I found the office manager, Laura, and asked, "Do you know if a Doctor Drita is supposed to be with my team today?

"The pediatrician? She finally showed up? Ya, Rose has been expecting her for a month," Laura said.

Only one week ago I had taken over the team from Rose, a petite redheaded German doctor who had been in Kosovo since the war began. She had worked with this particular team for the past six months. The staff had only one week to adapt to me as their new leader, and they were still adjusting to losing their beloved Rose. Now I asked them to accept another new doctor as well. Like people everywhere adjusting to change, they resisted the idea at first.

Packed like a tin of sardines, all three doctors, both nurses, a driver, and I squeezed into the van already filled with supplies. The tension in the tight van was palpable as we drove down the bumpy road to the village.

When we arrived at the *ambulanta*—a tiny, stark clinic without running water, Doctor Drita wandered off to find the bathroom. As we unpacked the van, the other four attacked me and prattled like children.

"It isn't fair!" complained Nurse Bedreji.

"We are too many," spat Doctor Mirvete.

"We are only women's care. Why do we need a pediatrician?" questioned Nurse Dejetare.

"We are already too crowded," whined Doctor Linda.

On and on and on it went, and this was only the part I understood. All four of the women spoke English. Doctor Linda and Nurse Bedreji continued to berate me in English. Frustrated, Doctor Mirvete and Nurse Dejetare shifted into Albanian. They were relentless!

I did the best I could to explain and apologize for not preparing them for the sudden change and then told them firmly I expected them all to help make Doctor Drita feel part of the team.

"Remember, we are MCH—*Maternal Child Health*," I reminded them. "Doctor Drita is here to help us with the child part of our job."

All conversation in the room suddenly shifted to Albanian. I think that one may have even called me a name, but I could only imagine what they were saying. Inwardly, I groaned. *Only one week in the country and already I'm the enemy. This is not a good beginning.*

I didn't understand why they so vehemently opposed the new doctor. Perhaps simply it was too many changes to accept. And they were accustomed to Rose. They didn't know yet if they could trust me. There is safety in a routine and comfort in the status quo. Because they had lived through a war, each of these women carried a long personal history that was more than enough to cause her to crave security and resist change.

Luckily, it was not a busy clinic that morning, and only one woman was waiting for us when we arrived. She was a thin woman with no upper teeth and only three lower, wearing a dirty white T-shirt, two sizes too large, and baggy black pants. She brought her five-day-old son swaddled up like they did their babies, like a little pig-in-a-blanket sausage. He was her third son. Her first two babies lived only one month. She felt certain they died of hunger.

"My baby is so big. My breast is so small," she said, hanging her head.

She asked for help to buy milk from a can for her baby, but we had no assistance of that kind, and, in fact, for a myriad of reasons, encouraged breast-feeding for all of our patients.

The antibodies that pass through to a baby in mother's milk alone are reason enough to encourage breastfeeding. Breast milk is also the perfect combination of nutrients for optimal infant health and growth. There is some thought that nursing helps with mother-baby bonding. There are other benefits for the mother too. Nursing soon after delivery helps decrease blood loss. It also helps the uterus return to its original size and tone, and it helps to lose the extra weight of pregnancy. Besides, it's free, and it comes already warmed in a clean container. There's no need to sterilize bottles, boil water, or worry if there is no money to buy formula.

Doctor Linda did the women's post-partum assessment and found the woman was recovering well and was healthy. Her only concerns were for her baby.

Both Doctor Linda and Doctor Mirvete tried to reassure her and tell her about all the advantages of breastfeeding for her baby.

They looked to me for guidance. I showed her baby positioning and encouraged nutrition and fluids. With the doctors translating, I assured the woman that her breast would produce all the milk that her baby needed, but I could tell by the nervous, tight, twitch of her body and the pinched expression in her eyes, she was not satisfied.

"Please help my son not die," she pleaded.

I felt a knot in the pit of my stomach as Nurse Dijetare translated her plea to me. Swallowing, I suggested it might help if Doctor Drita, the unwelcome pediatrician, examined the baby boy.

"Yes, the pediatrician!" said Doctor Linda, and then hurried off to find Doctor Drita.

It had to be Providence that brought this particular patient with her special concerns to clinic that morning because what I witnessed over the next hour was nothing short of a miracle.

Unlike the younger members on the medical team, Doctor Drita had not trained in the back alley educational system of medical schools held in basements and garages. She received her training prior to the unrest in her country, when institutions were intact. Doctor Drita was not just an adequate doctor; she was an outstanding one. With more than twenty years of experience and a passion and talent for teaching, she proceeded to perform the most thorough newborn baby exam I have ever witnessed. Anywhere.

Speaking in a low, calm voice, Doctor Drita slowly unwrapped the baby boy from his swaddling. Beginning at his head she gently palpated his fontanel—the soft spot on top on his head—and explained to the mother it should be soft but not sunken.

"This is one way you will know your baby is drinking enough," she told the young mother. "If his soft spot was depressed, it would tell us he was dehydrated, but see how nice and soft your baby's head is? Perfect!" Doctor Drita praised.

She gently palpated the baby's abdomen and pointed out there was no discharge, no redness, no swelling around his umbilicus—his bellybutton. "There should be no redness. No discharge. See how perfect this baby's tummy is? Perfect!" Doctor Drita said pointing to his tiny tummy.

As she continued to examined him, she explained every step to the mother and to the staff. She performed a neurological exam and demonstrated the "Dolls Eyes reflex"—a phenomena that causes a baby's eyes to open when gently pulled from prone to sitting position. Using another phenomena called the "Walking Reflex," she showed how he could "walk" when held in a standing position with his feet touching the table. As he lifted his legs in a stepping movement, Drita reassured the mother. "See, your baby is strong and well."

Drita was much more than simply an amazing doctor. She was a spiritual healer. As she demonstrated respect, patience, and kindness, the mother's ability to believe in herself blossomed.

The staff stood by engrossed as they learned how to properly evaluate a newborn. At the same time, and even more importantly, they saw the young mother's confidence grow before their very eyes. Her shoulders eased. The tight, pinched look around her eyes relaxed into a little smile.

When Doctor Drita finished with the exam, she re-swaddled the baby, placed him in his mother's arms, and instructed her to feed him. When the mother complied, Doctor Drita applauded. "Bravo! You see, your body will provide for your son."

It was a light-filled moment. All the doctors and nurses began to clap. The mother was smiling from ear to ear a wide, but toothless grin, and repeating, "*Faleminderit, faleminderit* (thank you, thank you) over and over again. Having Doctor Drita on the team was no longer a problem.

Miracles happen. They happen whenever, wherever there is great love. Bravo, Doctor Drita. Bravo!

SECTION FOUR

MANY TRUTHS, MANY WAYS

Socorro's Secret

"In Mexico, the foundation of a home is not the
earth, the foundation of a home is a women."

Mexican Proverb

She was a squat, round, dumpling of a middle-aged woman
with short, coarse hair that morphed into a new wiry shade every
week, first brown, then orange, followed by black, then back to
brown again with purple highlights added. I think Socorro was
experimenting with henna that winter.

From the heartland to the heart of Mexico, my husband, Norm,
and I came in search of a warmer perch that winter. We hoped to
catch a glimpse into the lives and traditions of our neighbors to our
south.

Having failed miserably a few years earlier at a weeklong crash
course in Chicago, I was also there to study Spanish. I thought
maybe if I came to the source and immersed myself, learning would
come easier.

Mornings were spent in the classroom with Socorro. Her name
means 'help or aid' in Spanish. What a perfect name for a teacher.
What a perfect name for Socorro!

We spoke only in Spanish. Not an easy thing to do when you
lack vocabulary, but Socorro made class fun with her sense of humor
and kind ways. She was demanding and strict but seemed to sense
when she had pushed a student too hard. She'd gently back away,
redirect the attention to a group participation project, tell a story
from her childhood, or talk about her son.

Socorro was short, barely five feet tall, and had a kind, round face and eyes that crinkled into slits when she smiled. She loved to play jokes on the students and the other teachers and tease about Saturday nights spent with her friend, "Don Julio," one of the better tequilas of Mexico. When asked on a Monday how her weekend was, she pantomimed drinking right out of the bottle, swaggered around the classroom, giggled, and whispered, "Don't tell. Our secret," with a wink.

Socorro was sincere, sensitive, and courteous, as were all the Mexican women I met while in San Miguel, but it went beyond mere politesse. Socorro cared deeply about people. She couldn't pass anyone on the street without stopping to say hello, inquire about their health, their children, their mother, and the rest of the family.

The difference from the cursory, "Hello, how are you?" greeting popular in the United States was Socorro actually wanted to hear how each person and their family was doing. She took time to ask. More importantly, she listened to the answers, then parted each person with a motherly hug before she bounced off again down the street. And Socorro did bounce. She was as tireless and buoyant as a rubber ball with only two speeds—standing still and bouncing.

After morning classes, we broke for a two-hour lunch, then returned to the school in the afternoon. Soccoro, or one of the other teachers, would accompany the class—a dozen students of various ages from the States and Canada—on field trips around town. The purpose was twofold: first, to teach us the history and culture of Mexico, second, to give us a chance to practice our new language.

Afternoons spent exploring San Miguel with Socorro were the best. She pointed out things I would have missed without her sharp eye leading and explained cultural nuances not included in a typical travel log.

When we took a field trip to *San Miguel Vieje*—Old San Miguel—just outside of town, we tromped down a dirt road, then across a dusty field to the original church built in 1542. We passed cows running loose along the way and pigs tied to scraggly trees. It seemed the pigs were more prone to running off than the cows. Old San Miguel, now a dusty little pueblo with a stone church and a few ramshackle little houses, was the original site of San Miguel de Allende.

"See this, Nancy," Socorro said, pointing toward something that reminded me of a roughly designed homemade barbecue structure made of stones and shaped like a beehive. It sat off to one side just outside the rock wall that surrounded the church courtyard. "Since before the *conquistadoros*," Socorro said, "*mis antepasados*, my ancestors, built this altar to the gods of the sun, rain, and corn. When the priests came to Mexico, they were smart. They built churches near the old places to worship. It made it easier for the people to accept their new ideas. The people of Mexico mixed the old ways and the new. We still do," Socorro said with a wink.

She showed me the small, empty stone room to the side of the church. "*Para la familia*," Socorro said. "For the family. The body is laid for viewing here when someone dies. The entire extended family comes and stays overnight. They celebrate the person's life, then the following morning burial takes place. The old church and the stone room are still used today.

"For us, Nancy, there is not so much difference in this world and the next," said Socorro. "They are the same. I have family here; I have family there. It is the same for me."

On another field trip we visited the open-air market, Socorro recognized one of the vendors, a middle-aged man with thick, straight, dark hair that fell casually over his forehead and gave him a boyish look. She sidled up to him. Talking in Spanish faster than I could follow, she chatted him up coquettishly and threw her head back and laughed at whatever it was he said. Soon he was cutting up pieces of papaya and avocado and offering them to us all. He offered a round purple-skinned fruit to me.

"What is it?" I asked.

"*Zapote Negro*," Socorro said, then quickly said something to the vendor.

He cut the purple fruit in half. Inside was a black, seedy pulp that looked like ground fig. He handed me half. When I started to taste it, he shook his head. Next he cut an orange in half and squeezed the juice over the black fruit I held. Orange juice ran down my hand. He smiled widely.

"*Comas*. You eat," he said.

I bit into the fruit. My mouth exploded with flavors, first sweet, then a pucker of sour. Orange juice ran down my chin and arm.

"This is my Mexico, Nancy," said Socorro. "This is the *sabor* of my Mexico."

Sabor means literally to taste, but it means much more. To *sabor* something is also to savor it, to steep in, to immerse yourself completely. I wanted to *sabor* all of San Miguel.

The colonial gem of San Miguel de Allende is nestled in the mountainous central region of Mexico. Local legend has it that a barefoot Franciscan monk began the town in the 1500s at the site of Old San Miguel, but the scarcity of water was an on-going problem. Then one day his hounds led Friar Juan Miguel to a stream a few miles away. He saw it was a much better place for the people to live and relocated the town.

When I was there, it seemed the progeny of those hounds were everywhere. Most residents had at least one or two dogs. Those watchdogs lived a restless life on the rooftops and kept watch over city.

Our life that winter took on a pleasant routine. Every morning I'd brew tea before heading off to school and take a cup to Norm, who would lie in bed and watch the *Hoy, Today, Show* in Spanish. Norm doesn't speak Spanish, but he'd try to guess what the news was. Then later in the morning he'd walk down to the *jardin*, buy a paper in English, and see how close he'd come.

The *jardin,* the town square, was the heart of San Miguel. It was a magical, picturesque park lined with Indian Laurel trees and filled with cobbled trails that wound past fountains and heavy wrought-iron benches where friends and family, young and old alike, sat and visited.

Everyone came together in the *jardin.* Beautiful teenage girls, accompanied by younger sisters, shy eyed and long lashed, came to meet gangly teenage *novios*—boyfriends. I saw the same courting ritual every weekend and came to wonder this: *was the older sister babysitting her younger sister, or was the little one along as a chaperone?*

The young women walked the perimeter of the *jardin* clockwise around and around. Sometimes they were only accompanied by the little sisters; often they walked in pairs with two little sisters trailing behind. The young men walked the *jardin* counterclockwise, usually in twos or threes. Their dance began with a smile, perhaps a greeting, then a few times more around and couples paired up magically. Soon the park was filled with young couples sitting on the benches under the Indian Laurels sharing a cup of cold corn covered in mayonnaise and white cheese, while little sister contentedly dangled her legs off the bench and savored the kiss of pink cotton candy melting in her mouth.

Every Saturday there was music. The Mariachi groups circled with their guitars and trumpets. Each group wore matching tight pants with gold buttons up the sides and short, cropped jackets decorated with gold or braid, and, of course, wide sombreros. For a small price they crooned love songs or mourned lovely laments of loss for couples or families gathered together.

Often a larger band played in the grandstand gazebo in the center of the park. The music usually started by 10 o'clock and everyone danced. I mean everyone.

Grandmothers twirled little boys, and little girls waltzed with their fathers by stepping on their feet and following. Young and old—local, expatriates, and tourists—joined in the bobbing mass of heads and feet in time to the music.

I appreciated the closeness of families and the way everyone, of all ages, partied together. It was different to what I was accustomed to in the States where after puberty begins children usually choose the company of their friends over family, and the idea of dragging a younger sister along on a date is not a consideration.

One Monday morning before class, Socorro and I chatted about our weekends. I mentioned how I loved the way everyone comes together for the dancing—all ages.

"Oh, yes, Nancy. That is the way of my Mexico. In my country, family is all. Family is my most important thing; after God, family," Socorro said in a serious tone. "My son? Maybe he comes even before God for Socorro," she finished with a grin. As always, there was more than a little truth to Socorro's humor.

I was taken by how gentle and helpful the local people in general were to me. It went beyond merely being polite. For example, one morning I asked directions to the *biblioteca*, the library, from a young mother with a dark-haired toddler in tow. The woman didn't simply give me directions; she turned around from the direction she was headed and led me four blocks to the library, a huge mustard-colored building with heavy wooden double doors.

When I thanked her, she replied, "*No es nada. Es mi placer, Senora.* It is nothing, senora. It is my pleasure."

I began to appreciate what it means to be truly genial. I wanted to live more like the Mexican women—to slow down, take time for people, really listen; I wanted to learn to be truly gracious.

Socorro was a typical Mexican woman, that is to say she was warm, sentimental, and caring. For Socorro, God came first. Then family, but family was close in the near tie for first place. Family was everything. My fondness for her grew daily. I loved hearing her talk about her life.

As an unmarried mother in macho Mexico, Socorro might have felt shame; however, never did she indicate that was the case. Her son was the spark behind her glow. She spoke of him often, always with great pride, and seemed happy that he came home from college every weekend with a bag full of laundry for Socorro to wash and iron. That was how she spent her Saturdays—doing her son's laundry and cooking for him.

"He is my love. He is my job," she said. "I work all week for my son's tuition. On Saturday I cook and wash and iron for my son, but on Sunday I rest. Sunday is for Socorro. Me and my friend, Don Julio, we rest," Socorro teased

When Socorro discovered how much I adore my grandson, she dubbed me with a nickname. The assignment was to write a paragraph describing a person. I turned in a lengthy diatribe about my grandson. Socorro laughed when I read it aloud and teased, "*Mama Cuervo,*" which means literally "Mama Crow." It is an expression used in Mexico for one who brags about their children or grandchildren. Socorro and I were *un par de cuervos del mama*—a pair of mama crows.

My studies and life floated that winter with ease. With so much to see, do, and learn, we were never bored. One of our favorite activities was to simply sit and watch life as it happened around us.

In Mexico, daily life is celebrated with gusto and Latino passion. My own Midwestern melting pot seemed watered down in comparison. Every day was an explosion of color. Fireworks were common. Flower vendors lined the *jardin* and sat on street corners with buckets of calla lilies, sweet smelling carnations and roses, and riotous bouquets of brightly colored zinnias. There was almost always at least one balloon vendor in the *jardin* with a rainbow cloud of shiny Mylar balloons above her head, so large it seemed it might carry her off in the breeze. Every day was a celebration.

But on this day I was not celebrating. I was sick. *Enfermo.* I coughed so much I couldn't sleep. I started antibiotics even though I knew they probably wouldn't help. I had a cold. Colds are viral. Antibiotics don't help. I knew that, but whenever I travel, I take medicine with me and take it readily. Odd, because at home I rarely take medicine for any reason.

When I disrupted class for the third day in a row with my coughing spells, Socorro took pity on me.

"Nancy, stay," she commanded as she dismissed the others for the morning break.

Oh dear. She's going to tell me to take my germs and go home before I make the whole class sick.

But Socorro only smiled, put a chubby arm around me, and pulled me close. Her head didn't quite reach my shoulder.

She looked up with a sympathetic expression and asked, "Nancy, you are sick?"

"Not really, I feel fine; it's just this cough. I can't stop. I'm sorry," I stammered.

"Do you want me to help?" she asked in a whisper, looking over her shoulder toward the open door as though checking to see if anyone were listening.

Intrigued, I wondered what she meant. How was she going to help me stop coughing?

"This is a secret. I trust you. They would not like it," she said, cocking her head toward the door. "You tell no one at school, okay?"

"Of course," I promised. This serious side of Socorro was one I hadn't seen before. She definitely had my attention.

"Who wouldn't like it, the other students?" I asked.

"No. My bosses. The owners would not be happy with Socorro if they knew what I am going to tell you."

"You can trust me," I promised.

Socorro gave me a little hug then bounced to the door and pulled it shut. With a mischievous look, she tested my language skills. "*¿La puerta es abierta o cerrada?*" The door is shut or open?

"*Cerrada.* Closed," I responded.

"*Bueno!* Good! See, you are learning, Nancy. The door is *cerrada*, like our secret," she said, pantomiming turning a key in the lock of her mouth. She motioned for me to sit down as she settled herself on a chair.

"What I am going to tell you I learned from my *abuelita*. You know *abuelita*?" she asked.

I shook my head.

"It is grandmother. *Abuela*, grandmother. *Abuelita*, my sweet little grandmother. Do you understand?"

"*Sí.*" I nodded.

"*Mi abuelita* was very wise. She had wisdom from her grandmother. I came from a long line of wise women. All *muy fuerte, muy sabios*—very strong, very wise," Socorro said, beaming. "*Mi abuelita* was *una bruha*—a healor. Some people say bad things about las bruhas, but they do not understand. *Mi abuelita* was a wise women, a woman with many gifts and great love."

"You are a lot like your grandma," I said.

"No, no. I am only Socorro, but *mi abuelita* lives inside me; in my hair, under my nails, in my bones; she is with me always," Socorro said.

She explained I needed to go home to rest for the afternoon. I was to take eight bougainvillea blossoms, boil them in two cups of water for five minutes. Then I was to drink the tea.

"Do it again and again. Drink as much as you can hold. Stay indoors after dark and don't breath in the night air," she said in an ominous tone. "Do you understand?"

Drink tea and stay indoors, is that all? I expected something more dramatic. "I do," I replied. "Thanks, Socorro. I appreciate your help."

"*En Espanol*, Nancy, *siempre en Español*. In Spanish, Nancy, always in Spanish," Socorro teased, slipping back into teacher mode. She bounced up from her chair and scurried outside to join the others drinking *café con leche* and munching dry vanilla wafers on the patio.

I gathered up my notebooks and slipped quietly through the

door. Walking home I pondered Socorro's advice. I expected something larger than a recommendation to go home and drink tea, albeit tea made of flower blossoms, but there certainly could be no harm in trying it. Socorro was mothering me. Maybe bougainvillea tea would do the trick that antibiotics couldn't.

I'll keep taking the Amoxol but add the tea to the cure. "*That which does not kill me makes me stronger,*" I chuckled to myself.

Arriving at my compound, I opened the large metal door and slipped inside. I picked the bougainvillea petals then coughed my way upstairs to make tea.

Eight blossoms, two cups water, boil for five minutes. Drink all you can hold. I heard Socorro's voice repeating in my head.

Maybe her bougainvillea tea would work, maybe not. It wasn't going to hurt to try it. It boiled down to only a cup. I let it cool and then gulped it down quickly. It wasn't unpleasant tasting exactly—something like Chamomile, but with a bitter aftertaste.

I lit the fire, pulled a blanket off the bed, and snuggled in on the couch for the afternoon, curious to see if the cure would take.

I thought about Socorro's advice to stay indoors. I had read about a malady the Mexicans call *Mal Aire*. It means literally 'bad air." It seems children and especially babies were particularly vulnerable to catching colds from it. That explained why even on warm evenings I saw children bundled up in coats, gloves, and hats, dressed as if ready to play in the snow. Babies were wrapped in layers and layers of blankets that covered even their heads. It was the Mexican mother's way of protecting her children. She swaddles them in love, just as Socorro was doing to me. She wanted to protect me from *Mal Aire*.

I dozed and woke when Norm returned from his afternoon at the *jardin*. He was excited to tell me all the things he had seen and people he'd met. The *jardin* was bordered with Indian Laurel trees trimmed to the shape of umbrellas. One of our favorite things to do was simply sit on a bench in the park and watch: a young mother and son fed the pigeons; whole committees of aging gringos solved world problems from a park bench; a woman served up cooked corn on the cob smeared with mayonnaise and cheese along with a cheerful "*Buenos Días*"; a young couple intertwined under the shade of a tree sharing the secrets of young love.

On this particular afternoon Norm talked to the large, baritone-voiced man who sold newspapers in the park.

"He speaks English?" I asked.

"A little, and we managed with some pantomime," Norm replied. "By the way, what are you doing home?" he asked.

I told him about Socorro's advice and recipe for tea. "She said her *abuelita*—her sweet little grandmother—taught her how to use her *tercer ojo*—her third eye—her intuition," I said.

"Just make sure it doesn't make you grow a third eye," Norm replied.

I made a face and sent him out to gather more blossoms. I was still coughing, but the first cup didn't seem to have hurt me. I'd continue to do as instructed. I'd drink as much as I could hold.

I returned to school the next morning. Socorro approached me on the patio before class. "You are feeling better, Nancy?" she asked.

"A little, thanks for asking," I replied.

"It takes time, Nancy. True healing must go deep and take time to be permanent. If you heal too quickly, your cough will return quickly. Remember. Drink as much as you can hold," Socorro said. I smiled and nodded.

For the next two weeks I drank bougainvillea tea until my teeth floated. My cold symptoms slowly abated. Every day I coughed a little less. I didn't know whether to credit the tea, the antibiotics, or just my own body's defenses to fight illness for my recovery.

I wanted to believe it was the tea.

I do know that I felt better each time Socorro asked how I felt, patted my arm, or gave me a hug. I also felt better each time I counted out the eight blossoms, added them to two cups of water, and watched the warm steam rise from the pan. I could almost hear Socorro whisper; *"Mi abuelita lives inside me, in my hair, under my nails, in my bones. She is with me always. I can help, but you must not tell. It is our secret."*

It's been several years since I studied Spanish in Mexico. I returned to my home in Iowa, where the only bougainvillea growing is a plant gifted to me by a friend. It lives in a pot on my patio in the summer and in my bedroom during the cold Midwestern winter. Now whenever I feel a cold or a cough coming on, I stay indoors after dark. I avoid the *Mal Aire*. And I brew up a tea: eight blossoms, two cups water, boil for five minutes.

I watch the steam rise from the teapot in a vaporous cloud and imagine a chubby, little, brown-skinned girl with a round, impish face, and eyes that laugh most of the time. Her hair, a wild halo of frizz, sticks out in all directions. She runs, never walks and laughs easily. She spies an old women coming down the cobblestone road. "*Abuelita!*" she calls.

The old women with a round, squat body has gray hair that sticks out like a coarse brillo pad frayed in all directions. She waves to the little girl and motions for her to come. The old woman sits down on a bench under an Indian Laurel tree. She pats the spot next to her.

The old woman asks about her day and listens carefully to the little girl's happy chatter as she answers. And the story of family continues. When the little girl has told her grandmother every detail, grandmother begins.

"Listen. I want to tell you about *mi abuelita*. She was a very wise woman, just like you will be one day. Listen closely. I am going to tell you of secrets."

$\mathscr{I}$ am a Curandera

"IT IS NECESSARY TO LISTEN, FOR GOD SPEAKS IN THE
SILENCES OF THE HEART."

MOTHER THERESA

$\mathscr{I}$t was one of those cold, drizzling, gray days with no promise
of sun to warm the frigid mountain air. My teeth chattered and I
shivered under my lightweight rain poncho. A huge droplet of rain
hit my forehead, rolled between my eyes, then dribbled down to the
tip of my nose. I wished I were somewhere else. Anywhere else.

A mixed group of healthcare providers on holiday under the
guise of continuing education, we gathered in this mountain village
in the highlands of Peru to hear midwives speak about their work.
The course was a study of alternative healing in South America.
From different parts of the world we brought varying degrees of
belief in any medicine, alternative or traditional, but everything we
had seen the past week had begun to change us. Even the most dis-
believing among the group was beginning to examine the possibili-
ties of another view of the world in the realm of healing.

A shroud of gray mist rose from the ground and the rocky, narrow road leading into the village. Chips peeling from the wall fronts
of gray stucco homes gave them a freckled appearance. Some of the
buildings were made from uneven handmade clay bricks chinked
with mud. A few roofs were topped with red clay tiles, most with corrugated tin, and a few with layers and layers of long grass thatch.

The rain slowed from the pummeling of early morning into the
soft spit and sprits common for mid morning in the highlands of
Peru. The sweet, musky smells of steamed corn mixed with the rain-

washed air. The women were cooking a feast for us. Guinea pigs scurried in and out of the kitchen where they lived until slaughtered for a special meal. Many would be butchered that morning.

We huddled together in a tight group sipping cacao tea from tin cups. We had been encouraged by our tour guides all week to chew coca leaves with an antacid tablet. The antacid added the calcium alkaline needed to extract the active ingredient from coca. When chewed together, it absorbed through our gums. It was supposed to be good for altitude sickness and seemed to be working. We were at thirteen thousand feet. Other than a few of us with mild persistent headaches, no one was sick. We waited to hear midwives talk about their work.

Two men spoke to us first and explained their work as midwives. I was surprised to learn men in this culture could be midwives. I had mistakenly stereotyped it as "woman's work."

We learned that often a *curandera* is called into the profession through a dream, their own or someone else's. It is equally common for the responsibility to be passed down from one generation to the next. Both of these men had been trained by their fathers, who had been trained by their fathers before them.

Each man told of similar practices, such as rubbing a woman's stomach with a urine-soaked stone for protracted labor and checking fetal position by reading the mother's pulse in her feet. As was the tradition, they cut the umbilical cord with a shard of pottery broken in the home at the time of delivery. I winced when I heard this, knowing of the risk for neonatal tetanus in a country where the mothers are seldom immunized against it.

Agripina was the last of the three midwives to address us. In contrast to the men who wore heavy beaded necklaces and brightly colored woven ponchos of hot pink, flaming orange, and brick red, Agripina was simply dressed. She wore a long, gray, wool skirt and dark green sweater. Her dark hair hung in a single thick braid under a gray fedora and fell almost to her waist. She sat quietly with her head bowed while the men spoke to us. When they were finished, she rose and began to speak in a quiet, soft voice. Her voice had a near mystical effect on the small crowd.

"I am a *curandera*," she said, and our guide translated. "I have been a *curandera* always. It was many years ago that a mother sheep told this to me when I had only eight years. It is not a thing I chose. It is a thing that chose me."

The crinkle of wet rain gear quieted. Those who had been moving about or rubbing their arms briskly in an attempt to get warm stopped moving. Her words were enough to pique my curiosity, but it was the sound of her voice—a low, melodious timbre—that held me spellbound. It had a timelessness and tranquility that seemed not of this world, as though an angel was speaking.

Glancing around the small crowd, I saw she had captured us all. The entire group leaned forward in rapt attention as though Agripina had something special, something precious to tell, and no one wanted to miss her message.

But a sheep telling her that she was a midwife? The doubting Thomas in my head questioned it. *What could she possibly mean by that?*

She went on to explain that when she was eight years old, her family had left her home alone for several days. She didn't explain where they went, or why, only that she was left behind to tend the small flock of sheep.

I tried to imagine leaving an eight-year-old home alone in the States. How frightening. How unsafe. How inappropriate and even illegal. However, in this more primitive culture, children are not children. They are small, responsible people doing their part within the family from the time they begin to toddle. It would not be so unusual that Agripina be left alone to tend the herd.

She told us it was not yet time for the lambing season. She would simply lead the sheep to the stream each day, once in the morning and again in the evening. In between they would graze. It would be easy. Besides, her family was not going far.

"They would go only around the corner and would return in a few days," she told us innocently.

Of course, we had learned this week that in Peru "around the corner" is an expression that may mean literally just that, or it could also mean a journey of many days. Time and distance take on different meanings for different peoples. One thing I was certain: Agripina's corner was not the same as my own.

"But," she continued, "even though it was not the lambing season, a mother sheep began to birth her baby. What could I do? My heart beat very fast. I looked, but I could see only one foot coming from the mother. She cried and she cried for so long, I became very frightened."

As she told her story, Agripina's eyes opened widely. She never changed her slow, melodic pace, but her speech became more intense. She had us hooked. We hung on the rhythm of her words and waited impatiently for our guide to translate her tale.

"What could I do? I was only a child. I had only eight years. But then the mother sheep spoke to my mind. She said, 'Help me,' and I knew what I must do. I took hold of that tiny foot, and I pulled and I pulled with all my strength. And the mother cried to me, 'Pull harder!' And I pulled and I pulled and I pulled until I thought my arms would break. But the baby lamb still did not come. My heart was pounding like a loud drum in my ears," Agripina said with wide eyes.

She paused, then began to smile as she continued, "A calm and peaceful feeling began to surround me. I no longer heard my heart beating in my ears. And I knew what I must do. In my mind, I said to the mother sheep, 'Don't be afraid. I am here. I will help you.' My mind spoke to her mind and she became still. She no longer fought me. She no longer fought her own body. Now two, tiny, wet, slippery legs protruded from the mother sheep. I took one leg in each of my hands. I pulled until finally a tiny, perfect lamb was born. And I knew then I am a *curandera*."

Everyone listened to Agripina's story in reverence. We could see in our minds a tiny brown-skinned girl with a single long braid pulling the baby lamb from his mother.

Agripina went on to explain that when her parents returned home and heard what had happened, they, too, understood her calling. She began then, at age eight, to train with her village's midwife. Over the years she continued to learn from the old healers of her village and the other villages nearby. Unlike the previous two midwives, who continued to practice exactly as their fathers taught them, Agripina has also learned modern midwifery and medicine from the nurses and doctors from other countries who visited her village.

"I am a modern *curandera*," she told us with a proud smile.

When the presentation was over, I made my way toward this

lovely woman. With the help of the guide, I explained I, too, was a healer, a nurse who worked with women and babies. "How can I help you? Is there anything I can send to you from my home in the United States?" I asked.

Shyly she smiled then reached into her bag and pulled out a roll of brightly colored hand-woven cloth. She unrolled it carefully and revealed a set of basic medical instruments—hemostats and scissors.

"I boil these in water for every delivery. Then the baby and the mother will not become sick. They are borrowed from a North American nurse. I must return them. I would very much like to have my own set of tools. If I had my own tools, I would never again need cut the cord with a piece of pottery," she said honestly.

Such a simple request. I purchased the instruments when I returned home and our guide took them back to the village six months later when the next tour visited.

Agripina will teach the next generation of midwives. She will continue to show them how to prevent sickness and even death for mothers and babies simply by using clean instruments at every delivery.

Agripina listens. She hears the whispered voices of inner wisdom we can all hear if we simply still our busy lives and listen. She is indeed a *curandera*. It is not a thing she chose. It is a thing that chose her when she had only eight years.

RAINBOW OF GLADIOLAS

"BE PATIENT TOWARD ALL THAT IS UNSOLVED IN YOUR
HEART AND TRY TO LOVE THE QUESTIONS THEM-
SELVES...PERHAPS YOU WILL THEN GRADUALLY, WITH-
OUT NOTICING IT, LIVE ALONG SOME DISTANT DAY INTO
THE ANSWER."

RAINER MARIA RILKE

I woke to the sound of church bells ringing, deep and sono-
rous; the toll resonated in my bones. I dressed quietly, careful not to
wake my tousled gray-haired lover sleeping peacefully on his back
through the ringing bells. A sheet thrown off in the heat of the
night lay in a rumpled heap on the floor. I tiptoed around it and
slipped through the door and into the street.

The village yawned and began to stretch itself awake. In the distance a rooster crowed and overhead sea gulls sang, *"Buenos dias,"* to
each other and to the fishermen in the bay below. A door slammed.
A baby cried in an upstairs apartment. The pungent smell of tortillas sizzling in hot oil competed with the fresh scent of sea air and
filled my senses with something sweet, musty, salty.

I padded silently down the nearly empty streets, ignoring the
rumble in my stomach. I would meet the gray-haired man later at
our favorite small café—*La Sirena Gorda*—such an endearing name
for a fat mermaid. I smiled and nodded to the baritone greeting
of the large man selling newspapers on the corner: *"Buenos dias,
senora."*

I loved the easy way Spanish rolls off the tongue with kind words,
tender, like warm, brown arms reaching out to offer a gentle hug.

Mexico's morning sun warmed my face as I strolled toward the small church I spotted a few days ago. At the corner two hand-some young men with straight, black hair and dark brown eyes sat smoking, hunched over morning coffee. "*Buenos dias, senora*," they greeted me politely.

"*Buenos dias*," I replied, nodding toward the young men, and then smiled as the odor of what they were smoking wafted by on a breeze, reminding me of younger days and other handsome men.

New to this village, I had no firm idea what time Mass would be held, but assumed, as in other cities and villages visited, it was likely any hour, on the hour, until noon.

I arrived at the corner of *Calle Ascencio* and *Cinco de Mayo* at a wooden structure painted white with a small cupola and a cross on top. The carved, wooden door opened easily when I tried the latch. I slipped through and into the welcome shade. With no priest or parishioners inside, the church echoed empty.

Out of a childhood habit, I dipped two fingers into the small ceramic font filled with tepid water, magically made holy by a priest's blessing. I made the sign of the cross, then wondered why.

Old habits die hard.

I tiptoed down the center aisle. My footsteps echoed in the still-ness, the hollow sound resonating as deeply as the bells that had called me out of morning's sleep. I recalled a little girl who loved to slip into an empty church and sit listening to the silence, especially when the hurtful sounds of home grew loud and the walls shook with anger.

In the small chapel, saints dressed in brighter colors than remem-bered from childhood days surrounded me. A bearded man in a bright red robe reached up in a beseeching gesture toward the ceil-ing. Another wearing turquoise bowed in prayer. I couldn't remem-ber any of their names—this rainbow of brightly colored saints lining both sides of the church—but easily recognized The Virgin Mary draped in vivid blue, her feet heaped with faded flowers, their brown-tinged edges curled from yesterday's heat.

I stopped at the third row of wooden pews, genuflected, and slipped into the pew and waited. For what? I wasn't sure. I never go to Mass at home. Only in Mexico do I feel compelled, drawn with equal pull by both the ornate cathedrals of the cities and the small, simple village chapels.

Why did I come here? Is it to steep in the spirit of a humble people as they celebrate Mass with such conviction of deep truth? Maybe I come seeking my own truth, my own personal version of what every conscious cell in my body already knows, but my mind has forgotten. Maybe I come hoping for something tangible to grab hold of, something to cling to until the slippery, mystic mystery diffuses into the half-filled center of my chest. I don't know for sure why I come.

The door behind opened. I heard someone come in, pause briefly at the font by the door—probably dipping fingers in the magic water and making the sign of the cross—then rustling sounds, like someone kneeling down on the floor.

An old woman's voice began to pray in a haunting tone—soft, but powerful like a harp's vibrations reaching into painful places I didn't even know I had. "*Dios Mio. Dios Mio,*" the old woman sobbed, her prayers continued, a long, tortured lament.

I'd never heard such a sad sound.

Then came shuffling noises from the back of the chapel as she crawled on her knees to the first saint, the bearded one dressed in red, and into my view.

She was an old woman with brown, weather-beaten skin, wearing a shapeless cotton dress, pale yellow with small faded-blue flowers, as though it had been washed often and worn for many years. Her hair was tightly woven into two long, gray braids that fell on each side of a hump that rose like an unwanted burden in the middle of her back. Her wrinkled features embodied profound suffering. Tears rolled like rivulets down the deep creases of her checks.

The old woman plucked a gladiola from the bundle of flowers she held in her arms. She laid the flower at the feet of the bearded saint and continued, on her knees, to the next statue, the praying man in turquoise.

Weeping, she bent over, a slow arthritic effort, and kissed his cold plaster feet, then laid a yellow flower on the floor beside the statue and crawled on. Each measured, agonizing movement chafed at my center. In empathy, I felt vulnerable, exposed, and raw.

The old woman continued to crawl forward, stopping at every statue, beseeching each with poignant pleas. Then, leaving a gladiola behind, she dragged on to the next statue.

She was oblivious of me sitting in the pew, a captive audience riveted by an old Mexican woman praying painful arias as she heaped brightly colored gladiolas at the feet of saints.

The sad lament continued. Tears ran down her leathered face and fell on the remaining flowers clutched to her breast.

She crawled humbly to The Virgin Mary at the front of the church. The statue, dressed in vivid blue, gazed down with a Mona Lisa smile on the old woman, as if listening to her heartfelt supplication.

"*Madre de Dios, Madre de Dios,*" she began softly, one mother beseeching another desperately, the words rasping a wretched crescendo as, one by one, she lay the remaining gladiolas, a rainbow of color, at Mary's feet.

I felt a spasm in my chest and realized I was holding my breath. I forced myself to exhale, but the vise continued to squeeze.

Leaving Mary's side, the old woman crawled to the baptism font in slow motion, wincing with every movement. She stood up slowly, gasping as she pulled herself up by the wooden edge of the font's base. Her hands now empty, she plunged them both into the font, cupped water in her palms, and ceremoniously doused her head with water three times, wetting the crown of her long, gray, braided hair, as she exalted, "*El Padre, el Hijo, y el Espiritu Santo.*" The Father, the Son, and the Holy Ghost.

I felt my chest squeeze even tighter. The gentle old woman's prayers had touched an empathic chord. At the same time, I felt the visceral prick of envy. The old woman was crawling through the flames, bravely sticking her head inside the lion's mouth. I envied such complete trust in bright-colored statues and, larger still, unconditional faith in things unseen. I held my own ideology in tight, logical control having discarded my faith, along with childhood innocence, a long time ago.

But there was something endearing and completely sensible in one mother asking for another mother's help. I considered that maybe not everything real can be seen, only felt, like a vise that squeezes your heart until it breaks. I heard my own voice, a childlike whisper, "Holy Mary, Mother of God, please hear her prayer."

The old woman prostrated herself on the altar beneath a gilded picture of a brown-skinned Christ, heart open for display on the outside of His white robe. She keened a heartfelt lamentation until, finally, catharsis complete, her prayers became soft sighs of acceptance.

The old woman slowly rose, crossed herself, "*El Padre, el Hijo, y el Espiritu Santo.*" She turned and shuffled back down the center aisle. Her face expressed the serene exhaustion of someone who has weathered a long, stormy night, but now sees the sky turn a hundred shades of wonder as day breaks.

Her footsteps echoed softly. She stopped at the door, dipped her fingers into the holy water and crossed herself, then opened the heavy carved wooden door and walked out into the bright sunlight.

I sat in the pew replaying the drama inside my head. I saw the old woman on her knees offering flowers to The Virgin. I heard her haunting voice beg, but beg for what? I understood only a little Spanish. I sighed. The language, like the little chapels, called to me. I knew I must learn more. I hadn't understood most of the old woman's words; but the essence, rich with meaning, penetrated my soul in a way that no lexicon, in any language, could describe.

The bells began to toll, grand and dolorous, announcing Mass to the villagers. I would stay. I would sit in the pew and bask in a humble people's spirit, and I didn't need words to explain how I felt.

The old woman knew in her bones why she came to the chapel that morning. She came to find peace.

I still didn't fully comprehend why I was pulled to the little chapels and cathedrals of Mexico, but I felt a connection to all the souls who have sat in my same pew, knelt on my same bench, wept with me at the feet of Mary. And I felt a connection to The Source of all things.

Maybe I am only searching for something tangible to grasp or hoping somehow the spirit of true believers will diffuse into my soul, or maybe it is simply that in another life, I was an old Mexican woman, with long, gray braids, carrying a rainbow of gladiolas in my arms.

SECTION FIVE

IN THE SHADOWS

$\mathcal{A}$ Somber Decision

"When motherhood becomes the fruit of a deep
yearning, not the result of ignorance or accident, its children will become the foundation
of a new race."

Margaret Sanger

"$\mathcal{I}$ was nine when Mama went away. First, she taught me how
to take care of myself, then she left," the tall, dark, sad-eyed woman
stated softly. "It was the year I started to bleed...down there...I
thought I was dying, thought I'd caught the cancer, but Sister Anne
said that I wasn't going to die. I would just bleed every new moon.
She said it meant I could have a baby now and that I shouldn't be
letting no boys be jumping up with me. But I was just a little girl,
and I didn't even know what she was talking about. I guess Mama
forgot to tell me about all that before she left."

The nearly six-foot, mahogany-skinned woman, Delores, told
me her story. I ran a clinic in her village in Southern Belize. Over
time she came to trust me but not at first. It began with baby steps.

First, she approached with questions about her daughter's health.
"My Lizzie, she got da louse," Delores reported one morning as I
unlocked the door to the clinic.

We went inside the shabby clapboard building together. Delores
looked around wide-eyed. She remarked it surprised her how clean
the clinic was on the inside. "It's clean," she said bluntly. "I know
that's a good sign."

I gave her a small bottle of special shampoo and a little comb.
She went home and carefully followed the instructions, washed her

little girl's hair and combed out the nits with the little comb. Then she washed all the bed linens and hung them in the sun to dry.

She stopped by the clinic the following week. "Lizzie carried on something fierce 'bout da combin', but da louse be gone now," she said.

Twisting a lock of her short, black hair nervously, her eyes darted around the room and avoided mine as she said, "My girlfriend...she don't want to make no more babies. Can you help her?"

She listened intently as if mentally taking notes while I explained all the choices of birth control her friend could choose from. I gave her pamphlets that explained how they each worked. Then we talked about "safer sex," and I offered Delores condoms. We practiced putting one on a banana. Delores blushed and giggled a little, but she managed to get the slippery condom on the banana.

"Now I can never eat another banana," she giggled.

"You tell your friend to come see me," I said. "I'd be happy to help her."

Delores took the handful of condoms I offered and put them in her pocket as she left the clinic. Much later, after we had become friends, she told me that as she walked up the road, still muddy from the last night's rain, she felt the little square paper packages in her pocket that each held a condom. *He'll never use 'em, and he'll be vexed if he knows I been talkin' to the nurse*, she thought, and threw the condoms in a pile of garbage at the corner of the street.

Finally, Delores came to the clinic for herself. "I don't want to have more babies," she said with a determined, set jaw. "I want to drink the pill."

Delores started stopping by the clinic two or three times a week in the afternoon while most of the villagers rested. She'd bring me an orange or share a soda and we'd sit on the steps outdoors and just talk. She seemed to enjoy the visits and appreciated the concept of confidentiality.

"You mean, it's like anything I say to you is just between you and me?" she asked incredulously when I explained it to her. "I haven't had anybody like that since my mama went away."

Gradually, Delores began to trust me and, little by little, she began to share her story. She was only nine years old when her mother went to the United States to find work. She left the oldest boy, seventeen-year-old William, in charge of Delores and her fourteen-year-old brother, Albert. Delores cooked and cleaned the house for her brothers.

For five years her mother regularly sent money home to the children. Then, without explanation, the letters and the money stopped coming. Delores didn't know if her mother was still alive. She remembered no father.

By fifteen Delores was pregnant. While receiving prenatal care from the Public Health nurse who came to the village twice a month, she asked, "What can I do to make no more babies come?"

Her question was met with holy wrath. The nurse told her all birth control was against God's will. She threatened to terminate Delores's prenatal care and take away her vitamins.

"She said I couldn't have the little red pills that helped me not be dizzy if I ever asked again," Delores said. "So I shushed up"

I believed Delores. Although it was not the official stand on contraception in Belize, individual practitioners were given free reign to assert their personal beliefs on patients. Another woman had told me a similar story only one week prior. When her village nurse found out the woman was getting contraceptive injections every three months at my clinic, she refused to give the woman's children their immunizations. In Belize there was no clear separation between Church and State.

One particularly hot afternoon, we sat on the clinic back steps, fanning ourselves to ease the stifling heat. Delores talked about when Lizzie was born and how happy she was. "I just wrapped my arms around that sweet baby girl and breathed her into me. And I made a promise that day that I wasn't never goin' to go away from my baby girl," she said.

Delores revealed she had been pregnant twice. "I was seventeen the second time it happened," she said. Then, in a gentle voice, with no hint of complaint she went on, "Lizzie's daddy was mad when I told him I was late—maybe I was pregnant. He said it couldn't be his, cuz he'd jumped up every time, and if I was pregnant then I'd been foolin' around. Then he thrashed me." Delores paused, her eyes filled with angry clouds. She shook her head as she mumbled, "Stupid man," and continued. "He never helped me with our baby girl, so I knew he wouldn't be helpin' me this time either. Granny had died and my mother was gone—probably dead too. William had gone to work in the United States, and Albert was in jail for selling ganja. I didn't have anyone. I was barely able to take care of Lizzie and me and she was just a baby still sucking my titty. I just knew I couldn't take on another baby. I just couldn't, and I didn't know what else to do."

So she traveled alone by boat to Guatemala with her eleven-month-old daughter. Abortion is illegal in Guatemala, as it is in Belize; but she had heard of a clinic there that was both clean and kind. "They might help me," she said.

Since keeping her secret safe was crucial, she pretended to visit a friend when she and her baby girl took the two hour bouncing boat ride across the huge bay to a foreign country where a different language than her own was spoken.

Once there, Delores took a taxi to where she had been told she would find the clinic. "I was so afraid when I first saw it. It didn't look like a clinic. It was just a rumply little shack behind a house with weeds all around…just a shack in the middle of a field. It made me feel real dirty when I saw it."

Delores hung her head and lowered her eyes. A lone tear slid down her cheek, then she raised her head and continued in a determined tone. "But I knew what I had to do, so I just got out of that car and I tells the driver, 'you come on back in four hours and don't forget.' He looked at me, and he looked toward the shack, and I knew that he knew and I felt so low I wished I could crawl under a bush."

Delores paused, looking ahead as if remembering the scene in real time, then turned, looked me squarely in the eye and went on, "Then he did the nicest thing. He reached his arm out the taxi window and fluffed Lizzie's hair and he looked at me and said, '*Buena suerte.*' That means good luck. Then he drove away."

Although it did not look like a clinic on the outside, once inside she found it spotless with tidy cots and clean sheets. "It had three cots and poles with bottles of clear liquid in them—just like a real hospital, and it had one of them tables like you've got with the things to put your feet in. I saw it sticking out behind a screen in the back of the room," Delores said.

"No one was there, just me and the doctor. She was an old white woman with gray hair—a long pigtail braided clear down her back. She was nice; she had little wrinkles at the corners of her eyes like people do when they've had an easy time and smiled a lot. She smiled at me and explained real simple what she was going to do. I knew then that the clinic was good."

As the doctor began to prepare her for the procedure, she placed Delores's feet in the stirrups at the end of the exam table. Delores panicked.

"I was so scared. I'm telling you; there are no words for how scared I was. I was afraid it was going to hurt. I was afraid my baby girl would be gone when I woke up. I was afraid my man would be mad if he found out and thrash me and give me a black eye like he did when I first told him I might be pregnant. But mostly, I was afraid God would turn away and never smile on me again."

The doctor assured her that her baby girl would be safe. "You'll just feel drowsy, barely asleep, and for only a few minutes. Don't worry, I'll watch your daughter," she promised.

When Delores woke up, Lizzie was playing happily at her feet. She felt a little cramping, but her nightmare was over. The doctor gave her medicine to make sure no infection developed. It was vital Delores remain in Guatemala until she stopped bleeding.

"I had to stay there until it was safe to go home. If I went back too quick and had a problem, like bleeding or something, they would make me tell who did it and then put the doctor in jail. If I didn't tell, they would put me in jail."

Delores stayed in Guatemala for three days. She had spent all her money for the boat, the taxi, and the doctor. There was none left to pay for a room. Delores slept fitfully in the alley behind the market, her sleep disturbed by the foul stench of garbage and the mangy dogs sniffing about out of curiosity and hunger.

"I was scared one of those raggedy dogs was going to bite Lizzie, so I covered her with my arms and unwound my hair. It was real long back then. I hid her under it." Finally, three days and three long nights later, Delores and her baby took the bumpy boat ride back home.

Fear kept her from asking anyone for help. It was essential no one learn her secret. She told her boyfriend she had been mistaken. She wasn't pregnant after all.

"I knew I could make him believe me. A man always believes what he wants to be true," she said with a little laugh. We both nodded.

Delores was completely alone with her secret. She couldn't even let the Public Health nurse in her village find out the truth.

"She wouldn't help me if I got sick, and she wouldn't give Lizzie her shots either if she knew. So I just couldn't let her find out. I couldn't let anyone find out," Delores said, then stared straight ahead in silence, as if lost in her memories.

She was only seventeen years old. She carried the burden of her dark secret alone for almost five years…until this afternoon when she shared it with an American nurse old enough to be her grand-mother as we sat on the back stairs of the clinic, drank colas, and tried to catch any small breeze that might blow off the water from the bay.

The day drenched hot, the air so heavy and thick that the birds wouldn't even fly. I discarded my white lab coat and wore only a red tank top over a flowered skirt this day. I mopped my forehead with a red bandana and waited quietly for Delores to continue.

"I can't sleep at night," she whispered looking down at her feet stretched out in front of her across the steps. "I'm scared to go to sleep." She went on to say she felt very sad. "It's not easy for me to smile." she sighed. Though her young face showed little emotion, her large brown eyes reflected a deep, lonely sorrow.

"What do you think about when you can't sleep?" I asked.

"He comes to me almost every night." Delores said softly, star-ing straight ahead. She continued as if she were seeing the scene in the blue water of the bay that spread out before us.

"He is a little boy and he looks about four years old, like he would be now, but his sound is like a new little baby's cry. He's dressed completely in yellow. He looks just like my little girl in the face, and his body looks real strong and thick, but his skin is yel-low…and wrinkled…like an old man about to die. My chest hurts when I hear him cry. I feel like my heart is cracking open," she whimpered.

Putting my arm around her shoulder, I nodded and silently offered my bandana. Delores moaned—a low, grievous sound. She began to rock back and forth. Over and over again she keened. "Like an old man about to die." I pulled her closer and together we rocked. We rocked and wept while a fisherman paddled his wooden dory in the bay before us and the sun slipped low in the sky behind.

Finally, Delores pulled herself upright and blew her nose into the red bandana. "I'm okay," she said. "Can I tell you the rest?"

"Of course," I said. "Please go on."

Delores said she had spoken to a very old woman, a friend of her deceased grandmother.

"Granny's friend has gifts. She knows about these things. I didn't want to tell her, but I wanted to know how to make the dreams stop. She says that my baby's spirit is not at rest because he stuck. He's stuck because he doesn't have a name. I think I need to have him christened. I've named him William in my head, but I call him Willie in my dreams. I think I'm going to ask the priest if he will christen him so he can move on to heaven. Then the dreams will stop."

Inwardly I sighed. I wished I could comfort her. I wanted to pull the six-foot, long-legged girl-women onto my lap and hold her and rock her until her tears stopped flowing and the sad dreams stopped haunting her nights. But all I could do was listen. Listen and acknowledge her feelings. Listen and affirm Delores's difficult decision. Listen…and know in my bones; to merely listen fell completely short.

I had an idea. Could we do a naming ceremony right here in the clinic? It could be just Delores, her granny's friend, if Delores wanted, and me. We'd come back tonight, when the clinic was closed, and do a blessing ceremony for William.

"What do you think?" I asked.

Delores stood, wiped her eyes one last time, and handed my red bandana back with a timid smile. "Thanks," she said.

"Keep it, I've got another" I said.

"No, I mean thanks for listening to me. I haven't had anyone's ear like that since Mama went away," Delores said.

She went on to say she would think about a naming ceremony. I sensed it would not happen. A plainspoken, white-skinned nurse from Iowa just couldn't grant the absolution she needed.

Delores stood up, brushed the wrinkles from her shapeless flowered shift, and sighed softly. "I think I gotta go tell the priest."

NORMA JANE

"MAN IS THE ONLY ANIMAL THAT LAUGHS AND WEEPS,
FOR HE IS THE ONLY ANIMAL THAT IS STRUCK WITH
THE DIFFERENCE BETWEEN WHAT THINGS ARE, AND
WHAT THEY OUGHT TO BE."

WILLIAM HAZLITT

Ricardo stood in the airport waving a sign above the jumble of people rushing about. I just had my suitcase rifled by a smirking, dark-skinned man with narrow eyes. The others in our group, five professionals from the Midwest traveling together on a cultural exchange to Guatemala, were in separate lines going through Customs. They were having their own underwear and socks tossed about the airport.

Eventually, I stuffed my belongings back into my suitcase, had my passport stamped, and passed on into the waiting area of the airport. It hit me with a jolt—bustling, hustling movement all hurry-scurry. Everyone seemed rushed to get in or out. Even the language was too fast for my limited Spanish. Dazed, I looked around, relieved when I saw Ricardo wave his placard with the name of our sponsor organization printed in red. We'd meet under his sign once everyone had cleared Customs.

Ricardo, a retired American with gray hair, but a young, virile quality, had lived in Guatemala for nearly fifty years, during which he worked for an American non-profit agency. He was our local contact person. He and his wife, Norma Jane, would be our leaders for the next month.

He gathered the five of us together and surveyed our mountain of *equipaje*—suitcases—one of the few words I could remember from my weeklong crash course in Spanish. He grabbed a suitcase in each hand, shouted, "Follow me," and raced toward the door.

We clutched our belongings and stumbled after him in single file like a row of ducks following their mother. I brought up the rear pulling two suitcases on uncooperative rollers behind me. The drive that followed through unfamiliar neighborhoods was a blur.

Norma Jane opened the door and welcomed us into their home with a lop-sided smile painted in tangerine lipstick running above her lip line and toward her cheek, like elderly women so often do. After quick introductions, Ricardo excused himself to make calls to our sponsor host families. He would arrange for us to be picked up after dinner.

The home was a simple block construction with large, high-ceiling rooms. The living room was clean but very cluttered, magazines and books piled everywhere. Norma Jane pushed a stack of *Good Housekeeping Magazine*, circa 1960s, off the couch and motioned for us to sit while she chattered nonstop.

"So happy to have you all here! I wish one of you could stay with us, but you know—the plumbing—it just wouldn't work. Ricardo said no—you'll love your hosts though. Lovely families— well, I don't know some very well—but Ricardo does. He knows everybody! We'll be taking you to the Highlands! I get to come along on that ride. Oh my! That will be something. We'll shop in Chichicastenango. Do you know about Chi-Chi? The shopping is the best. Maybe we'll visit the church. Interesting place. Kill chickens right on the steps before Mass. You know about the chickens?" Norma Jane prattled nonstop, barely coming up for air. Then she stopped suddenly and said, "I need to cook. Excuse me." She wobbled away in the direction of the kitchen.

My mind spun from the word salad she had just tossed up. Her speech was clear, not slurred, but something about her was "off." The nurse part of me speculated. Perhaps mental illness or an anxiety disorder?

It wasn't until later, while I helped her in the kitchen, that I realized it was not complicated. Norma Jane was simply drunk, but she was delightful, not the least bit obnoxious like some can be, slobbering and spitting out mean-spirited remarks.

A large water glass full of dark red liquid sat on the counter.

Norma Jane was busy making authentic Guatemalan soup. The kitchen was filled with the insipid odor of black beans cooking when I entered and asked, "Can I help?"

"Come in! Come in!" she said, taking a large gulp from the glass. "Oh my yes, I never have help in the kitchen. Here, you can stir." She handed me a large wooden spoon and pointed toward a pot of black slurry simmering on the stove. Between each step of the recipe, she took a gulp from the glass. *Chop-chop-chop* the carrots. Gulp of the red. "Now where did I put the garlic?" A gulp of the red. "Stir deep. Don't let it stick." Gulp of the red.

While we cooked, Norma Jane asked about my home in the States and life in general. Then, in a wistful voice, she told me about her children. She had two, a daughter and a son, raised in Guatemala, but now both lived in Texas.

"Oh, how I miss them," she said. "I miss home terribly, but what do you do? Ricardo likes it here, so we stay. I've been here most of my life. We came here back in 1956. Ricardo's work, you know? I just never thought we'd be here so long." A gulp of the red.

I tried to imagine what it would be like to live here for nearly fifty years. I understood this wasn't the life she had imagined as a young bride when, in support of her husband's career, she had moved to Guatemala. She expected they might stay a few years. Now, a lifetime later, she was still here. And she was still homesick.

She fell silent while she chopped onions with a vengeance. Tears slipped down the creases in her wrinkled face. I sensed not only onions caused those salty rivulets. Norma Jane was tipsy sweet—a heartrending tipsy sweet. Her world turned topsy-turvy. She drank to forget that all she wanted was to go home.

Soon the soup was ready, and we sat down to our first meal together in this county so unlike our own. Over the meal Ricardo laid out what adventures might unfold over the next month. Our host families would collect us this evening. We'd sleep at our host homes, but every day we'd gather together for a month packed with cultural events, clinic and hospital observations, industry tours, museums, and visits to primitive villages. During the middle of our stay, he and Norma Jane would accompany us on a road trip into the Highlands. There we'd have a peek into indigenous life of the Guatemala Maya.

The next two weeks were a blur of excitement and color. Exhausted, I looked forward to a slower pace in the country. Ricardo and Norma Jane picked us up in the morning. Ricardo drove a large van to accommodate the seven of us and our luggage. We looked forward to the adventure ahead—The Highlands!

I had only seen Norma Jane once since the evening we arrived in the country. I sat next to her at a ball given by our sponsor organization. Norma Jane and I were both underdressed at the elegant party. I had come unprepared to attend such events. My travel wardrobe included only simple clothing. In my plain, black, short dress, I felt out of place in a room full of suits and glimmering, long, formal gowns. Norma Jane wore a white native shawl with heavy embroidery. She told me it was called a *huipile* and was the traditional dress of Guatemalan Mayan women. Each village has its own designs and colors of embroidery. Her red cotton skirt had a border of bright embroidery around the hem that fell just above her bare sandaled feet.

Norma Jane and I bonded that night in the comiseration of hapless misfits that showed up for the prom dressed in cotton. We laughed and chattered together about our coming road trip. I looked forward to it enormously. It seemed the highlight of Norma Jane's year. While we chatted, Ricardo moved around the hall, talked with the men, and danced with slinky-gowned women. He didn't ask Norma Jane to dance. She sat on the sidelines where I suspected she spent most of her life.

A few days later we left for the road trip. We traveled together for a week. Every day Ricardo told Norma Jane where to sit. The placement seemed to reflect his mood. On a good day he'd instruct her to sit in the front with him, but if, as on this particular day, he wore an unhappy scowl and snapped, "That's enough," stopping Norma Jane's chatter mid-sentence, she got banished to the back where she shared a seat with me.

As we pulled into a lakeside town, Norma Jane told me that she used to live here. "I didn't like it, but Ricardo did. He worked here for years. He knows the whole town—too well." she said. The bitter pause that followed suggested there was more to that story.

The explosion of color that burst from both sides of the street lined with *tienda* after *tienda* selling weavings—neon hammocks, blankets, place mats, and tablecloths—detracted me from our conversation. In my mind I was already scoring a bargain—maybe a hammock—as bartering was so much more fun than single-priced shopping in the States.

Suddenly, Ricardo slammed on the brake and jolted me out of my bartering daydream. The van bucked to a stop in the middle of the road. He leaped from the vehicle with more agility than expected of a man his age and ran toward an attractive woman walking down the side of the street.

"Carmelita!" he called out. The woman with loose, flowing, dark hair around her shoulders, dressed simply in a white blouse tucked inside a dark, full skirt, was at least thirty years younger than Ricardo.

She appeared surprised, then pleased, to see her old friend. Ricardo took her by the shoulders and held her gaze for a long moment—longer than felt comfortable to those of us who followed the scene through the van's dust-smudged window. Slowly, the polite kiss-kiss, cheek to cheek, the customary greeting in this country, then Ricardo slid his arms possessively around her waist as her arms encircled his neck. I was unable to look away. Time froze in the van as we watched silently, a private moment that seemed to go on forever.

Ricardo's hand slowly slid down Carmelita's skirt and came to rest low across her bottom. He gave a squeeze, then a playful slap and slowly pulled himself away. The two old friends stood apart on the road, but their eyes continued to drink deeply.

My own cheeks braised pink. I felt guilty for my own voyeurism, embarrassed by Ricardo's disrespect for Norma Jane, shamed by what the scene might indicate. No one said a word; the van screamed with silence.

Slowly, Norma Jane turned away from the window. She dug into her purse and rummaged until she retrieved a tarnished gold compact and a tube of lipstick. With trembling hands she carefully applied the lipstick and then pressed her lips together. Hard. She snapped the compact shut, and with a sad, crooked, tangerine smile, faced straightforward, head held high.

AMID THE CHILDREN AND CHICKEN

"HISTORY, DESPITE ITS WRENCHING PAIN, CAN NOT BE UNLIVED, BUT IF FACED WITH COURAGE, NEED NOT BE LIVED AGAIN."

MAYA ANGELOU

As we passed through the Serbian village of Partes, peacekeeping guards were at checkpoints on each end, but with our humanitarian organization's logo on the Land Cruiser, we could go through without stopping. I waved to the young American soldiers. My driver, Burim, scowled.

"They are here to protect the Serbs," he grumbled.

Yes, indeed, the soldiers were there to keep the peace. And what an uneasy peace it was.

Burim had been assigned to serve as my driver, bodyguard, and translator. Little by little throughout the days we spent together, he shared his own personal version with me of Kosovo during the past ten years. Before the NATO bombings, when the ethnic cleansing escalated, he and all of his family, except his mother, fled to Turkey, where they lived with relatives. His mother stayed behind to protect the family home. They felt that she, as an elderly woman, would be the safest from harm from the Serbian Army. They stayed in Turkey for three months while NATO forces pummeled their homeland with bombs in an effort to drive out the enemy—the Serbian Army.

As we lurched down the bumpy road driving towards his own mountain village, in search of patients that need to be driven to the hospital for blood tests, Burim relived his trip of returning home from Turkey.

"We came together on the bus that was bringing many of us back to our Kosovo. We did not know what we would find, but as we passed house after house along the road burned out by the awful Serbs, my father began to cry. With each house we passed, he cried harder and harder. My father no longer cries. Now, my father cannot work. His spirit is broken. His heart is cracked," Burim said quietly.

I wondered if his father was clinically depressed, but didn't press for details, only nodded. As Burim continued, his jaw jutted forward in a determined manner as a tear trickled down his sweet young cheek.

"The next time I will not go away. I will fight to my death," he hissed.

His eyes narrowed and he squeezed the steering wheel fiercely in a white-knuckled grip, and then shook his head, as if to remove the memory from his mind.

We rode on in silence. There was nothing I could say that would ease his pain or make it better. I could only listen. I could only nod my head to indicate I had heard him and respect the silence that followed.

Nearly everyone I had met since coming to Kosovo had a distressing, horrific story. And they bore a fervent need to have their story heard. Within minutes of meeting, women who spoke English launched into the shocking details of the atrocities done to them or to their families. Even those who didn't speak English, upon learning I was American, quickly found someone to translate and shared their stories with me too. Everyone needed to express his or her grief and pain, to have it witnessed by another person. And it seemed particularly important to the people of Kosovo for an American to hear what had happened to them. They were enormously thankful we rescued them from the atrocities that had been escalating over the previous ten years.

I recognized the importance of each person being heard. I understood that the mere process of the telling validated their experiences—made their story real. The telling was a necessary step to begin to heal. However, I had heard more gruesome details than my middle-aged Midwestern mind could support over the two months I had been in Kosovo. I began to shut down. I detached. I could listen only with my ears.

Arriving in the village of Sllatina, we soon located the first patient after making only one inquiry at the tiny local store. When we arrived at the home, a large two-story building with an enclosed courtyard, there were many children playing among a flock of chickens. They ran forward with wide smiles and grabbed me by the hand. I couldn't understand their chatter, but I did catch the word "Americana."

We explained to Mirvete that she must come with us to the hospital for a blood test. She quickly, and it seemed even happily, agreed to come. Maybe just the opportunity to get away from her seven children, ages seven months to nine years, plus the three nieces and nephews that lived there, was reason to celebrate a trip into the city. She retreated into the house to get ready, and as she did her mother-in-law stepped out the door.

She was an old woman with a tired, weathered face and bright, carrot-red hair peeking out from under her wool scarf. The day was dry and the hot winds had been blowing for more than a week. I wondered why she wore a scarf in the heat. She shook my hand profusely and began talking to me in Albanian, the words tumbling out without stops between her sentences. I gathered she was thanking me.

"*Faleminderit Americana.*" Thank you, American.

The Albanians felt with all their hearts that the NATO forces saved their lives because the daily atrocities did not stop until NATO bombs fell.

The carnage had begun more than a decade earlier, when the Serbian Yugoslavian Army overthrew the government. First, they threw all Albanians out of government positions. Next, professional positions, such as in medicine or education, came under their control. It was mandated that all university courses be conducted only in the Serbian language as a deterrent to Albanians becoming educated. Eventually, they were not even allowed to attend the universities at all.

But these insults were minor compared to the systematic "ethnic cleansing" that went on. Serbian soldiers burned homes and raped the daughters and wives of Albanian leaders. Sniper shootings became an everyday occurrence and pipe bomb explosions were common. These efforts escalated severely during the year before NATO became involved. The Serbian goal was to kill or drive out all Albanians from the country and that effort did not stop until the West intervened.

While the NATO forces were made up of soldiers from many countries, the Albanian people seemed to give the United States most of the credit for ending their ten-year nightmare. "*Faleminderit Americana!*" I'd heard it often since I had arrived in Kosovo, and it always made me feel so proud to be an American.

The old woman with the carrot-red hair continued talking, and in a desperate, pleading tone that stretched the strings of my heart to near breaking, she began to lament on and on, but I didn't understand. I asked Burim what she was saying.

He replied simply, "She wants to tell you about the war."

Another nightmare to expose…another story that must be heard, I thought to myself. Everyone I met since arriving in Kosovo had a nightmarish memory of horror they needed to share with another human being. As the country and its people began to rebuild their lives, it seemed not only by telling, but also in having their own private stories heard—really heard—that broken lives were somehow validated.

Inside my head I thought, *I just can't listen to one more sad story*. Inside my heart, I knew I must. Perhaps in the telling, this old women could begin to heal.

The old woman wailed and squeezed my hand. The intensity of her emotion escalated.

"Please tell me what she is saying," I asked again. And this time Burim translated.

"Many people came here to hide and escape from the soldiers… There were more than two hundred living here then, but the soldiers were more, and they came and they beat my sons." The old woman began to cry as she told her story. Huge tears ran rivers down the creases of her tired, wrinkled face. "I begged them, 'Please, do not kill my sons, but they knocked my sons to the ground and kicked them…and kicked them…and kicked them…There were many young women. The soldiers took the young women into the barn and . . ."

The old woman continued to tell her story; violent words plummeted from her fierce mouth; however, Burim stopped translating. His lower lip and chin jutted forward, his face turned to stone. The woman continued on relentlessly in Albanian; however, I needed no further translating to imagine the horrors she was relating.

While I wished there was something that I could do that would ease her unmitigated pain, I could only listen. Listen, with my ears and my heart, to bear witness for her story.

I opened my arms and there we were, two grandmothers, from opposite sides of the world, cheeks wet with tears. We stood in a courtyard in the middle of the Kosovo countryside among the children and the chickens and shared a memory too poignant for words.

SECTION SIX

EARNED WISDOM

You Are the Nurse?

"No love, no friendship can cross the path of
our destiny without leaving some mark on it
forever."

Francois Maurie

The day marked my fourth month in Belize. My husband, Norm,
and I had spent weeks and shed buckets of sweat turning a dirty,
dilapidated corner of a building into a medical clinic. Since then,
day after day, for long hours I attended to patients while geckos
climbed the walls and termites built fresh trails on the ceiling over
my exam table.

Though I was a nurse, my duties had expanded beyond providing basic health care. I also disposed of the occasional dead rat on
the path to the clinic, swept mounds of dead bugs from the floor,
and waged daily war against mosquitoes big enough to ride. Once,
I even armed myself with a machete and battled an opossum that
wanted to make my clinic his home.

But on the day that marked my fourth month in this tropical
country, I was taking a much-needed break from work. For one day,
at least, I would be Nancy the Photographer and not Nancy the
Nurse.

The pick-up truck bumped down the winding road that would
take Norm and me out to the countryside. In the pre-dawn darkness,
the morning breeze felt refreshingly cool. I knew that the heat of
the day would soon leave me drenched with my own perspiration.

It was the dry season, and although we passed towering fan
palms and the thick understory beneath the tall trees of the rainforest, the road was parched and dusty.

The truck jerked along over deep ruts in the road as we made our way to the village. I had arranged to spend the day with a young woman named Terese. Judy, an American teacher from New Hampshire, introduced Terese to us a few weeks ago.

We took a trip to the next village to deliver books Judy was gifting to the small library she had built for the village. After the books were shelved, Judy took us to the school to meet her friend, the teacher, Peter.

The school was a large rough-cut lumber structure with bare wood floors and open windows. Barefoot, brown-skinned Mayan children crowded two and three to a desk. While the town of Punta Gorda's population was a diverse mix of all the ethnic groups of Belize—Creole, Garifuna, East Indian, Mestizo, and Mayan—the small outlying villages seemed to be only Mayan with each village being either Mopan Maya or Ketchi Maya. The classroom had few books. It was a typical village school in southern Belize.

What was not typical, however, was the computer sitting on the teacher's desk. It seemed the children might have the advantage of learning computer skills, or, perhaps, even Internet access, I thought naively.

Later Judy explained the computer was a gift from a church in the States, but since the village had neither electricity nor telephone lines, the computer was on display simply to show the children such things existed.

"We'll get electricity in our village someday," was Peter's positive take on the matter.

Judy had been coming to Belize on school breaks for years. She had many friends in the villages. On the way back to Punta Gorda she asked if we might stop in the next village over. She wanted to buy *jippa-jappa* baskets, and she knew of a family in San Miguel who she had bought from before.

A woman sat under a tree in front of a rough-cut lumber hut—with a palm frond roof. She wore a pale green cotton dress, the bodice trimmed in bric-a-brac in the traditional style of the Mayan women. Her long, dark hair was parted in the middle and pulled back into a tight bun at the nape of her neck. She stood up as we approached on the dusty road and walked barefooted to the truck. Judy introduced her to me as Terese.

Terese remembered Judy and became excited when she understood we were there to buy baskets. She immediately ran into the hut and returned with an armful of small baskets, hand woven from strands of the *jippa-jappa* plant.

I was particularly impressed with how well Terese spoke English. English is the official language of Belize and the language that is taught in all schools. However, in the small villages it is not unusual for only the men to speak or understand English, as it is often not considered important for little girls to attend school. The native languages of Ketchi or Mopan Maya are commonly spoken. Sometimes in Belize it seemed the language was a mixture of English and their native language. The mix was particularly confusing and difficult to interpret. However, Terese was easy to understand.

"Do you prefer the large ones or the small?" she asked as she held up an armful of baskets.

I choose a few small baskets. Then, entrepreneur that she was, Terese suggested she could make any size basket that I wanted. "A special basket just for you," she said.

I ordered one the size of a large mixing bowl and we settled on the price. It would be ready in two weeks.

Next I asked Terese if, when I returned to pick up the basket, she would consider allowing me to spend the day with her. I wanted to observe and photograph her life and would be happy to pay her for her time.

She giggled and asked, "You want to learn to make baskets?"

I explained that yes, I would love to watch her weave baskets as well as anything else she typically did as she went about her daily work.

"I want to record a day in the life of a woman in your village," I said.

Terese seemed both shy yet excited about the idea. We agreed on a price and arranged a date. That was two weeks ago. This morning, without a telephone or any other way to confirm our plans, I wondered whether my visit would be welcomed.

"Do you think she remembers? What if her family isn't as enthusiastic about my spending the day as Terese seemed to be?" I fretted to my husband as we neared the village. "You'd better stay at least until I make sure this is going to be all right."

As the truck lurched up to the small grass-thatched hut, I saw that my concerns were unwarranted. Terese and her entire family—mother, grandfather, two sisters, a pack of little boys, and two babies—were all waiting by the road with wide smiles.

"Hello, Miss Nancy," Terese called out as I stepped from the truck. "I so happy you come. I so afraid you no come."

Turning to my husband, I grinned. "Worrying over nothing, I see. See you back here before dark?"

"You bet. Enjoy your day off," he said. Then he disappeared back down the road, leaving a cloud of dust in his wake.

I came to the village with an agenda: to play, not work. While nursing is my vocation, photography is one of my passions. I was eager to capture the distinctive beauty and culture of Belize and its native people on film. I planned to spend the entire day, from dawn to dusk, photographing Terese and her family as they went about life in the rainforest.

As they began their day, I observed the well-choreographed bustle of daily work. Most efforts involved food preparation for the mid-day meal, with all family members pitching in. I marveled at both the rustic simplicity of their life and at how creative they had been in adding modern "technology" to lighten their workload. For example, to grind corn for tortillas, Terese replaced the traditional flat rock and pestle with a hand-powered grinder much like the one my grandmother used to grind meat. She boasted that her new grinder made her work much easier and faster. It now took only two hours to prepare the cornmeal and make the tortillas for lunch.

Once the corn was ground, I helped Terese and her sister, Justina, gather the laundry and carry it down a dirt path to a small creek that ran behind their home. All eight little boys of the house, ranging in age from three to ten years old, accompanied us. On the way I tried to memorize their names and identify who were Terese's sons and who were Justina's. I learned that one of the children was actually Terese and Justina's brother.

There were no technological advances for washing the clothes. Just as their ancestors have done for hundreds of years, the women simply laid each piece on a flat rock, rubbed it vigorously with homemade soap, rinsed it in the creek, then wrung it out with their hands before placing it in a large handmade basket. Standing in thigh-deep water, Terese and Justina scrubbed each article of clothing carefully, taking great pride in how clean the clothes became.

Crouched like little monkeys, the boys lined the creek bank to watch the women. They seemed to be waiting for something. When the laundry was done, the women walked out of the water and wrung their dripping skirts onto the ground. Terese nodded at the boys, and the frenzy began.

They peeled off their clothes and jumped into the water. Laughing and shouting, "Watch me! Watch me!" they performed a show of underwater handstands, jumped from the creek bank over and over again, and swung from a rope tied to a tree high above, landing with a splash in the creek below. Such pure joy! I found myself laughing along with them and was tempted to shed my clothes and join in the fray.

Soon though, we headed back toward the house. There was more work to be done. The huge basket of clean laundry was carried back to the hut atop Terese's head and then hung on the line to dry.

Next, Terese weeded the garden using a pointed stick and machete. I helped her dig and pull weeds from around tomato plants, yams, and chilies.

"If we don't do this every day, the forest will eat the garden," she explained solemnly. I was surprised to find no corn in her garden, but Terese said the men could bring corn home from the fields.

While photographing the family going about their normal routines, I realized that everyone did their part with little or no discussion or instruction. They each seemed to know their respective role in the lively choreography of their daily life. Even the little boys returned after their morning swim to cut grass with sharp machetes. What had at first looked to me like the playful attacking of grass with their "weapons" soon turned to hard labor that caused tiny beads of perspiration to form on their little foreheads.

Later that afternoon, we sat crouched on low stools outside the thatched hut in the shade of the cashew tree, resting and chatting. Occasionally, the soft afternoon sounds of a birdcall or cricket were heard. The morning work was over. Children were bathed, laundry washed, garden weeded, yams dug, corn ground, tortillas cooked, the black hen killed, plucked, and boiled.

We had filled our bellies with the simple food and now was the peaceful time of day, the siesta, when the children played quietly and the women sat undisturbed, enjoying a few moments of female companionship and tranquility.

"You are the nurse?" Terese asked hesitantly.

"Yes," I answered, also hesitantly, reluctant to return to nurse mode just yet.

"For my sister—you have medicine to make no more babies?"

I smiled to myself. For my sister…how many times have I been approached since coming to Belize with that question prefaced by "for my friend, for my sister, for my cousin"?

It was easier for most women to ask for someone else, more difficult to own their own questions. The question was, in fact, the real reason I had come to Belize. The primary purposes of the Women's Clinic were to improve women's health and offer modern methods of family spacing.

And so we talked. I learned that, at age twenty-four, Terese had four children and that her sister, Justina, twenty-six was the mother of five. They had many questions and misunderstandings, which soon poured out.

"If I drink the pill, I will catch the cancer," Justina said.

"The injection—will it make me crazy with sex? Will I want many men?" Terese asked.

I had heard these same misunderstandings about contraception from other women who came to my clinic. The pill would cause cancer, injections increase the libido dramatically, and my personal favorite, "If a man jumps up (withdraws) then I won't get pregnant."

I talked with Terese and Justina and tried to dispel each of the myths. Then I explained not every method of contraception, but the choices available in Belize at the time—the Pill, injections, IUDs, and condoms. We talked. We laughed. We talked some more.

When Grandfather stepped outside the door to see why we were laughing, their talk quickly changed to the art of making *jippa-jappa* baskets.

"We gather the leaves from the forest," Terese said, "and then we boil them for hours until only the spines are left. Then we hang them in the sun to dry."

"They must hang for many days if it rains," Justina added, picking up the conversation.

"Once they are dry, we begin to weave. Each basket takes many hours. A large basket maybe days," said Terese.

I appreciated that Grandfather was not to know their secret. Only when he reentered the hut did our talk resume. Perhaps the idea of family spacing was too modern for grandfather to accept. His generation had babies whenever they came—usually about a year and a half apart thanks to breast-feeding's temporary natural contraceptive effect. And contraception implies one has a sex life. I think granddaughters everywhere, married or not, hesitate to admit it to their grandfathers.

Terese and Justina are a new generation who will bridge the centuries between pounding clothes on a rock and using modern birth control. Both agreed they wanted "to make no more babies," and, unlike the patient teacher who waits for electricity to arrive in his village someday, Terese and Justina wanted control of their fertility *now*.

I felt like Margaret Sangor floating diaphragms into the New York Harbor in whiskey barrels as I arranged for the women to walk ten kilometers to my clinic during their next moon time. They chose "the injection." They smiled. They sighed. They seemed so grateful, it more than made up for all those wretched mosquitoes, rats, termites, and opossums.

As dusk approached, we heard the sound of Norm's truck approaching. My day in the life of Terese was coming to an end. I would never forget her, or her sister, Justina. They each hugged me good-bye.

"We will come see you soon," Terese promised as she hugged me hard and long.

"I so happy you come," said Justina as she hugged me good-bye.

Then the entire family—all sixteen of them—followed me to the truck and waved good-bye as we drove off waving our own good-byes and left San Miguel village in a dusty cloud.

When I reflect back on that hot, dusty afternoon in a remote village in the middle of the rainforest, I am filled with gratitude. Not only do I have the wonderful photographs, I have marvelous memories of the day I sat under a cashew tree with two lovely young women and witnessed the power of simple conversation to change women's lives.

We talked. We listened. We laughed. We made a connection.

 Mermaid's Bounty

"IF YOU LOOK AT WHAT YOU HAVE IN LIFE, YOU'LL
ALWAYS HAVE MORE. IF YOU LOOK AT WHAT YOU DON'T
HAVE, YOU'LL NEVER HAVE ENOUGH."

OPRAH WINFREY

A long-legged, slender woman stood in the cockpit of her sail-boat. Silver streaks glinted in her light brown hair. "I prefer to think of it as minimalist," she said, wrinkling her nose, folding her arms across her small chest. She turned a frosty shoulder away. I knew immediately I had said the wrong thing.

For nearly a month my land-loving husband, Norm, and I, her closest friend, had lived aboard Janet and Joe's forty-two foot sloop, *Cabiri.* We sailed the winding coast of Panama, stopping nearly every day at a different cove or beach to stretch our legs, hunt for shells, and explore. On *Cabiri* quarters were a little cramped, but for the most part, it was working.

One morning as Janet climbed out of the galley and handed me a mug of steaming, black, strong coffee, I described the image of the sky at dawn—morning's mango sun rising as the apricot crescent moon falls.

Janet laughed and said, "What's with all the food imagery? I must not be feeding you enough."

But she was -- feeding me that is -- especially my spirit, and although our meals were simple, we certainly had all we needed.

Jan's slim, long-legged, athletic build lends itself well to the cruising life. Sometimes she has to climb fast to loosen a stuck sail or move quickly to reel in one set of ropes and reef out another simultaneously to jibe against a forward wind. Sailing takes both strength and agility. A lifelong athlete and former marathon runner, Janet was well suited for living on a boat in lots of different ways.

She taught me that to survive on a sailboat you have to be ever vigilant, watching the horizon in all directions for other boats and floating debris. Janet's tightly wired, mildly anxious nature, coupled with her eagle-like vision, made her the perfect lookout, especially during night passages when the sky and the sea turn the same shade of indigo-black.

Only a few days before she had taught me how to call dolphins by kicking her heels against the side of the boat. One of the leaping pearl gray animals poised mid-air and looked Janet straight in the eye as she leaned over the side of the boat—a freeze-framed instant—each acknowledging the other in a millisecond of recognition and respect. A dolphin knows a mermaid when he sees one.

How idyllic it had sounded when Janet first invited us to share their sea-life for a month. We would tour the coast of Panama on their sailboat, *Cabiri*, named after the Greek gods that protect sailors at sea. We would explore coves and beaches, collect seashells, and swim among brightly colored fish.

As wonderful as it had been, however, the reality of living sequestered was taking its toll, especially on the days the wind blew too hard to kayak to shore. Much of the time I was held captive in the cockpit because of the waves of nausea that washed over me each time I tried to go below deck.

I suspected Janet, too, was growing tired of living so close-quartered and sharing her small *Cabiri* space. It isn't easy to share your home, not even with your closest friend.

I watched Janet wipe clean a small piece of saran wrap and carefully fold it, saving it for a future use. "You live very frugally on the boat," I observed, the words slipped out without forethought, intended as an honest compliment.

Janet didn't find it flattering. "I prefer to think of it as minimalist," she said, turning a chilly shoulder. Tight-lipped she moved away, ducking through the guy wires like a ballerina executing a graceful arabesque as she climbed to the front of Cabiri—"forward," as she called it—and sat down on the bow.

What is it they say about company after the first three days? Was

I starting to smell like a sierra fish? *But life is lived frugally aboard Cabiri*, I stubbornly insisted to myself. That isn't an insult. Nothing was ever wasted, and isn't that what frugal means?

I admired the creativity we used aboard the boat to make sure we had everything we needed. We were living what I called frugally, but the word meant something else to Janet.

Inside I sighed. I had picked the wrong word. It obviously hit a nerve. Now we'd move apart for a bit. Janet at the bow trying to find some piece of air that was her own to breathe; me in the aft puzzling over what it was that I'd said.

Later we'd come together. One of us would apologize. This time it was my turn; or, we'd simply make a joke and hug it away. Solid, seasoned friends, Janet and I easily forgave each other. Frequent hugs and phrases like, "I am so glad you're here," were often heard.

But this time, the tight wire of tension stayed taut all day. The "F" word hung balanced on a slender line that stretched between us. Jan nursed her bruised ego on the forward bow; while aft, the committee in my head held stubborn panel discussions on the definitions and descriptions of the word "frugal." We went to bed that night with hugless curt "good nights," each pretending nothing was wrong.

I tossed and turned in my narrow cockpit berth, unable to find a comfortable position—the one that would relax my stiff-necked guilty conscience and let me fall asleep. Sometime in the middle of the starry night, lit by a crescent citron moon that could hold water, I abdicated the chair position of that debating team in my head. Definitions and descriptions aside, I had hurt my friend's feelings, and I needed to apologize.

Janet is not unlike many women met through my travels—women who live with very few material goods or the comforts of what we call modern living. Women who could be described as living in poverty, if their lives weren't so rich and abundantly full with relationships, nature, and Spirit. I appreciated Janet's minimalist life; I admired her for living the way she did. I hadn't meant to hurt her, but I had with my poor choice of words. I needed to put things right between us.

The following morning I cornered Janet in the galley. "Hey, I didn't mean to insult you yesterday. I'm sorry." I said. "I just meant…

well you know…to describe how you get by with so little here on Cabiri. I meant it as a good thing…but, I guess I didn't say that very clearly."

"I know. But I do like the word *minimalist* better," Jan replied in her soft voice. "I like not using more of anything than I really need. It's like with the water. When I think about the long showers I used to take, I almost feel ashamed. It's just so wasteful. It's just wrong! I like living minimally, using the very least of everything that I can, and it's a good thing because living on a boat it has to be this way. It's almost like a game for me to see how little I can get by on… well, maybe more of a religion." She smiled wryly. "Frugal sounds," she wrinkled her nose and shook her head with a little shudder, "I don't know…stingy? I just don't like that word. These four years living on *Cabiri*…well, it's taught me something. It's taught me that I have everything I need…and…what I need is enough. Do you understand?"

I nodded to indicate I did understand Janet's sage philosophy. Then my long time friend put one arm around my neck, bumped our foreheads together, and said, "I'm so glad you're here." And the tight wire of tension relaxed into that easy, familiar chain of friendship that has held us together for almost twenty-five years.

Only a Nurse

"It is not how much we do. It is how much love we put into the doing."

Mother Teresa

Picture it: You are in a small, sparsely equipped clinic with no electricity or running water in a mountain village. You arrived here after lurching down a bumpy, winding road into the green hills freckled with bright red poppies. Purple lupine-like flowers line both sides of the road.

Besides the trunks full of medical supplies, the van is stuffed with people. A driver, you, and three jerry cans full of water crowd the front seat. Your Kosovar staff—two doctors and two nurses—are packed four abreast in the backseat. Medical supplies fill the remaining space behind, piled nearly to the ceiling.

A pastoral slideshow plays out through the side window you are crushed against. Sheep graze in a meadow, peasant women with orange scarves tied behind their necks weed fields with wooden hoes, a boy in baggy britches, held up by wide suspenders, stumbles behind an oxen pulled plow. The scene gives no hint of the recent war. It's easy to forget it ever happened. Then you pass the winding barbed spirals of razor wire sprawled among the red poppies that mark the territory of the KFOR base—the Peacekeepers—here to protect a tenuous peace, and you, and every other person riding in the van, remembers.

We were headed to the village Halabok to staff a medical clinic for women. The concept of seeing a doctor throughout a women's pregnancy was new to this country so full of contradictions—on one hand as modern as my own Midwestern home, on the other as backward as the Dark Ages.

My job was to teach the staff how to provide basic prenatal care. Women's healthcare had not been part of their medical training. The humanitarian organization I worked for had begun the training program eight months earlier. Now we had only four months left to finish.

Our patients were mostly pregnant women, or other women with reproductive problems or seeking contraception. We used large garbage bags to form privacy curtains and examined two women at the same time, in the same room, by the light of a hand-held flashlight. We performed the exams on makeshift tables, or on a blanket spread on the floor. We washed our hands with water poured from a bottle brought with us and then shook them dry. The *ambulanta* (clinic) had no supplies. We carried everything we needed in two large army lockers.

On the way to Halabok, we stopped in another village and bought pastries they call *brioches* and warm yogurt for breakfast. I was becoming used to eating yogurt warm; however, I hadn't gotten accustomed to the greasy pastries filled with cheese, potatoes, or, my personal un-favorite, tuna fish.

Doctor Guli commented she felt carsick from the winding road. I offered to trade places in the van. Dark-eyed, pretty Marika sat next to me in the crowded van for the hour drive out to this particular village. She was tall and thin with a dark mane of wild hair that circled her shoulders and tumbled toward her face. She nearly always held her head bowed, eyes downcast. Her dark eyes held weariness unnatural for one so young. I had never seen her smile. In the short time I had been in Kosovo, I had not yet had the opportunity to talk to her alone. Sitting shoulder-to-shoulder next to her in the van this morning, I tried to strike a conversation.

"Marika, when did you decide you wanted to become a nurse?" I asked.

She turned toward me and answered solemnly, "I was a little girl. I was eight years old."

Her hollow tone suggested there was more to her decision than just a little girl's dreams; however, she did not elaborate. I felt a sinking melancholy settle around my shoulders like a dirty, ragged shawl.

"Do you enjoy working in the villages?"

She nodded her head then asked, "Is it a good thing?"

"Is what a good thing—nursing?"

"No, I mean do you think it is a good thing that we go to the villages," she answered.

"Hmm, I think it's a good thing. I think what we do in the villages helps the mothers and their children," I said. "How do you feel about it?"

Marika paused, then answered slowly. "Maybe, it is a good thing now, but what about when you and all the others go? What then will happen?"

I sensed this was not a casual question. It was something that had weighed on her for some time. It reflected her own lack of confidence in her nursing skills, but larger still, reflected doubt in her country's healthcare system.

Medical training in Kosovo was less than adequate by Western standards. A nurse's training consisted of a high school diploma. Doctors attended the same high school followed by only four years of university. Reproductive health was not part of their curriculum. Furthermore, medical training for the Albanian Kosovor doctors had been thwarted by political unrest over the last decade. During that time they were forced to develop a separate, parallel system of both medical education and healthcare provision. The fact that medical school was taught, literally out of homes and garages, is a shining tribute to the strength of spirit, resilience, and tenacity of these wonderful people.

I knew Marika's concerns were legitimate but tried to put a positive spin on the situation. "Marika, when we leave, you will still be here, and you and the others will continue to care for the women in the villages."

"But I am only a nurse. There is little I can do!" she exclaimed, eyes widening as if I had suggested something outrageous.

I grasped her forearm firmly. "No, Marika, please, never, never say 'I am only a nurse.' There is much that you can do already and a lot more that you'll learn, but really the most important thing any of us can do for our patients is to simply be there. Be there. Do you understand what I mean by that?"

Marika simply turned away from me, lowering her head until that cascade of black curls blocked her face from my view. She gave a slight shrug. Inwardly I sighed and felt that dirty, ragged shawl grow a little heavier over my shoulders. I wondered, with morbid curiosity, what grim experiences had stolen this young woman's joy.

We had held clinics in this village every month for the past five months. By now the women expected us. So when our van rumbled into the courtyard, they were already overfilling the small hallway that served as a waiting room.

We saw them one by one—old women wearing *burkas*, or long skirts, and their heads covered with scarves, young women in faded cotton dresses or Jordache running suits, likely donations from the many churches and other organizations that sent aid after the war. The women's clothing, like so many things in Kosovo, seemed incongruent. Some things were as modern as any part of Europe; others felt like time travel back a hundred years.

No one seemed upset by the two- to three-hour wait. In fact, each woman seemed incredibly grateful that we were there. I contrasted this to the reaction I would get at home should a patient have to wait so long. Grateful is not the word.

I worked with Marika gathering medical histories from the women. The thirty-fifth, and last patient of the day, was doing well herself.

"But there is a woman in her village who has labored for three days. She is asking can we help?" Marika translated.

We tried to glean more information about the laboring woman, but she wasn't very helpful with details. Nurse Marika translated as the woman repeated over and over, "So much pain. For three days, so much pain."

Since we had seen all the patients, we closed the clinic early and drove to the nearby village to assess the situation. Perhaps we could help.

There, in a tiny, run-down house nearly bare of furniture, we found a thin young woman named Hamide with her mother-in-law and five little waifs dressed in threadbare clothing. The children ranged in ages from two to eight. The oldest, an eight-year-old girl, stood at the head of the bed and watched soberly as I examined her mother.

Hamide was in hard labor and, just as her friend reported, she had been contracting for three days. The good news was she wasn't bleeding, her bag of water was intact, and most importantly, the baby's heart rate and rhythm were strong.

Because she had no money to pay, Hamide had been afraid to go to the hospital. The real tragedy was that since the war, and the changes in government, the hospitals no longer charged pregnant women anything. Maternity care was now free. But neither she nor her husband was aware of these changes. They only knew of earlier times under the harsher Serbian rule. Hamide had suffered three days for nothing.

Leaving the five children in the care of their grandmother, we loaded Hamide into our van and headed down the bumpy road to the nearest Health House. A Health House is similar to what we would call a small rural hospital in the United States.

Marika sat next to Hamide with one arm wrapped protectively around her shoulders, the other gently stroking her forearm. "*Ju lu, ju lu*. We are here," she whispered over and over.

I was grateful Marika was there and wondered if "only a nurse Marika," realized how valuable she was on that bumpy ride to the Health House.

"*Ju lutem, boor!*" Hamide cried out.

Marika translated, "She wants her husband."

Hamide was concerned that her husband, Abedin, might be angry with her for going. He, too, worried about having no money to pay. Luckily, we passed him walking home from working in the fields and were able to take him with us to the Health House.

I was amazed he had gone to work with his wife in her third day of agonizing labor, but with five other children to feed, this father and husband was doing the best that he could. Besides, birthing was women's work. He left his mother in charge.

Hamide seemed relieved when we found him. Between contractions, she thanked us profusely.

"*Falemenderit. Falem*enderit. Thank you. Thank you," she whispered. It was a forty-five-minute drive to the Health House in Podujevo, and as we bumped along the road, Hamide's contractions increased and became even more intense. She bore them bravely though, making only low guttural sounds as the waves of pain washed over her thin, frail body, while Marika, seated on her left, held Hamide's hand and gently stroked her forearm. On her right sat a tearful Abedin. Marika translated as he urgently pleaded, "Do something, please! Please help my wife."

I wasn't expecting that she would deliver before we got to the Health House. With the history of three days in labor, I guessed that there was a problem of Cephalo-Pelvic Disproportion. That's medical jargon for either the baby's head is too big, or the mother's pelvis is too small. At any rate it wasn't going to happen. This baby needed to be born surgically. I assumed Hamide needed to deliver by cesarean.

From where I sat behind him, I noticed beads of perspiration on our driver's neck. "It's okay, Tony," I whispered and squeezed his shoulder gently. "She's going to be all right."

I held a quick discussion about what everyone's role would be should an unlikely delivery take place on our way to the hospital. Tony sped up even more. As we careened down the gullied road bumping from side to side, we all shouted at him to slow down before we all ended up in the ditch!

Everyone listened wide-eyed as I gave instructions and tried to appear composed. I wanted to instill in them confidence I didn't possess myself right at that moment. I remember telling them, in what sounded like an unusually calm voice, "I don't expect Hamide to deliver her baby before we get to the Health House, but we need to prepare, just in case. Please don't worry, I have done this before. We can do this together."

What I didn't mention was that each of the three babies I have delivered was in a hospital setting when the doctor didn't quite make it in time to catch the baby, but did show up just a few minutes later. In short, I was faking it. Inside my chest there was a pounding that went clear off the target-heart-rate charts. Tony wasn't the only one sweating in that van as we skidded down the bumpy road to Podujevo.

Marika continued to comfort Hamide. She reached into a bag of supplies, pulled out a cloth diaper, and asked Doctor Guli in the front seat to dampen it from the jerry can of water. Then she gently wiped Hamide's face and held the damp cloth to her forehead. All the while she continued to whisper softly, "*Ju lu.* We are here."

Before you think that we ended up delivering a baby on the bumpy, winding road, let me tell you that we did make it to the Health House in time. However, because we were already late getting back to headquarters, we couldn't stay for Hamide's delivery.

The war had left behind a shattered infrastructure. Telephones were non-existent or unreliable. We couldn't call in to report where we were and, as so often was the case, the radio in the van couldn't reach the office either.

Although the war was officially over in Kosovo, there was still a lot of unrest and violence occurring daily. Late returns were not allowed for our own safety. If we didn't leave immediately, the security staff would be sent out to look for us. Tony promised to return to the village and deliver a small package of baby clothes, gifts from the team, for Hamide's baby.

The following week he reported that Hamide had a healthy baby boy, delivered by cesarean, and both mother and baby were doing excellent. She promised him she would bring her baby to our clinic when we returned next month.

On that summer evening we left the Health House together just as sunset cast a rosy glow over the winding road that led back to the city. We felt quite proud and jokingly dubbed ourselves "The Emergency Maternal Medical Team" and teased Tony about being our ambulance driver.

Marika, the young, somber nurse who that very morning had questioned what she, only a nurse, could do for the village women, hugged me, and I saw her smile for the very first time.

As we climbed into the van, she announced in broken English, "I think inside me we did a good thing today. I am happy. It is good that we were here today. It is good we could be for Hamide"

CHOICES

"LIFE CAN STRETCH YOUR SOUL OR TEAR YOUR SPIRIT.
YOU CHOOSE."

THE ORANGE SELLER

The screen door banged behind me as I left the house. I was up early, but already the sun had risen like a ripened mango. I stood on the porch, stretched, and yawned. The crisp smell of the sea stirred me awake. Roosters crowed in the distance, and overhead birds soared in the air with a variety of songs and calls. From an open window came a baby's cry, and down the street a door slammed shut. Punta Gorda Village was coming alive.

I trudged down the road, past clapboard shanties with peeling paint, or no paint at all, making my way to the fish market. Tall, wild grasses edged the road, along with fragrant, bright red hibiscus and dawn-tinted bougainvillea. No breeze stirred the damp morning air or fluttered the palms along the roadside. At the corner I turned and headed toward the waterfront. Three skinny, mangy dogs rooted through the garbage bunker searching for their breakfast.

As I made my way down the road, muddy from the previous night's rain, I passed a man plucking a freshly slain chicken in his front yard. His white teeth flashed against his dark brown face, and his black eyes danced mischievously. He smiled and raised his prize by its wrung neck. Inwardly I shuddered, but smiled and called out, "Now that's what I call fresh chicken!"

I was becoming more appreciative that the food I ate was alive—

recently alive! I cringed as I recalled that the evening before my husband had found a whole chicken foot inside his tamale at dinner. Here there was no waste. All food organic, all precious, but sometimes the experience so visceral it left my senses painfully raw.

That morning, my Iowa home and Midwestern ways seemed so distant. I felt a flicker of homesickness. *You're a long way from Kansas, Dorothy*, I quipped to myself and reflected back to the events that had led me to this tranquil little town.

In 1997, I was given the life-changing gift. I participated in an international professional exchange program. My view of the world enlarged. I took a hiatus from work in the States and came to the rainforest of Belize.

The village was a quiet little place, where life lumbered along at a slow pace and gave a sense of stepping back into a time when women washed clothes with a bucket and a scrub board, children played safely outdoors long after dark, and people really knew their neighbors.

This morning I was headed for the fish market, a large, stark, concrete structure the size of a garage with an open doorway and two windows, furnished only with one crude, wooden table for displaying the fish. The front faced a road lined with palms that ran along the waterfront; the back opened only feet from the beautiful turquoise bay.

When I arrived, I sat on a cement bench off to one side, basked in the warm sun, and watched the sunlight dance across the water in front of me. I breathed in deeply and exhaled with a peaceful sigh, because I knew there was no reason to feel hurried. Time was viewed differently here. Ideas, like schedules or set hours for stores to open, simply didn't exist. The fishermen might return at eight o'clock a.m. or maybe not until noon. I knew it would be awhile.

Meanwhile, inside the fish market, women gathered and gossiped, speaking in their own guttural languages of Creole and Garfuna with shrieks of infectious laughter spreading through the group. I wandered inside, and I found myself laughing along with the women, feeling strong and centered. Although I didn't understand what they said, I felt in my bones it was contraband and part of that shared mystery and bond of womanhood—girl-talk.

Near the doorway an immense black woman in a straw hat

bedecked with a bright red flower sat carving oranges. She sold them for a shilling, which meant a quarter to me. They weren't a bargain because they only cost ten cents at the produce market, but no one seemed to mind, and the orange came not only peeled for me with a smile, but with some words of wisdom.

"Life can stretch your soul or tear your spirit. You choose," her rich, melodious voice advised as she handed me the sweet smelling, sticky orange.

The children came with their mothers to buy fish. They ran about helter-skelter, playing tag. There was a festive feeling in the air of this daily gathering while we waited for the men to return.

When the fishermen arrived, the crowding began. It was first come, first serve, and everyone wanted fish for dinner. With very little conversation among themselves, the strong, dark fishermen unloaded their dories and brought the fish inside on long stringers. They piled them in a heap on the wooden table. With scales glistening, some of the fish lay motionless in the hologram heap, unstaring eyes wide open; others quivered and shuddered, their gills pulsated in dying gasps.

Men in dreadlocks weighed the fish and sometimes offered to fillet it for the women.

On one corner of the table, an old woman battled with a large fish that just wouldn't die. She whacked it on the head several times. *Whack! Whack! Whack!* When she began to scale it, it jumped off her table. Angrily she snatched it back and savagely bludgeoned him again and again.

Only the children and I reacted. We stood mouths agape; repelled, yet at the same time riveted by the brutal kill. When the children crowded close to the old woman, she yelled and waved them away, muttering and cursing like a gypsy witch.

She gripped the fish firmly with one hand and clutched a knife in the other. She scraped vigorously. I ducked to miss the flying fish scales, but they hit me in the face anyway. I recoiled. The stench of fish filled my nostrils; my stomach turned.

I came to the village as a volunteer. I wanted to do my own small part toward making a little piece of the world a better place, but in all honesty, I came with a selfish motive too. I wanted the adventure of enmeshing myself in another culture and experiencing it with gusto, using all of my senses. I wanted to distill from the adventure a depth and grace that was missing in my life.

Some days I was able to open myself completely to the experience. Other days, like this one, I found myself shutting down, closing off and missing home where fish came to me frozen, already breaded, in a box and chicken was a skinless breast on a Styrofoam platter wrapped in cellophane.

I came to the fish market to experience all its textures, smells, sights, and sounds. And I came to buy fresh fish for dinner, but watching that fish be pounded to death stole my appetite. A wave of homesickness echoed deep through my bones.

I walked back up the road toward home. The orange-selling woman's sage words repeated softly in my head. "Life can stretch your soul or tear your spirit. You choose."

I passed a group of schoolchildren on their way home for lunch. I waved to them and they called out in unison, "Good day, Miss Nancy!" I plucked a red hibiscus from a plant beside the road, inhaled its sweetness, and put it behind my ear.

And at that moment, more significant than the day itself, I chose. Yes! In my bag I carried a fresh sea bass I knew I couldn't fry for dinner. I'd need some time to forget the sound—that terrible *Whack! Whack! Whack!* Nevertheless, I lived in the rainforest, the sun rose like a giant mango at dawn, birds sang a halleluiah chorus, and the children called my name.

Indeed, it was a very good day.

APPENDICES

Opportunities for Action

BELIZE FAMILY LIFE ASSOCIATION

The Belize Family Life Association (BFLA) was founded in 1985 and is the only private not-for-profit organization in Belize dedicated primarily to reproductive health. BFLA has six health services centers. In addition to these centers, BFLA has established an outreach program using mobile nurses who travel across the country providing family life services in areas that are not easily accessible. To increase the scope of its program, BFLA trains volunteers, teachers, and community leaders to act as educator. For more information see www.ippfwhr.org.

Belize Family Life Association
2621 Caribbean Shores Mercy Lane
P.O. Box 529
Belize City, Belize
Central America

GUATEMALA FUND TOMORROW/AK TENAMIT

Project Ak Tenamit is a community development organization located on the Rio Dulce river in Eastern Guatemala. It is dedicated to empowering indigenous communities through programs in health, education, and family income generation.

When Ak' Tenamit was founded in 1992, the villages had no access to basic services, such as medical care or education. Today, they provide the area with education, healthcare, and community development, while supporting the sustainable use of national park resources.

They are empowering their communities by improving access to basic healthcare, education, and alternative income sources. To learn more see www.guatfund.org.

The Guatemalan Tomorrow Fund
P.O. Box 3636
Tequesta, Fl 33469
USA

INTERNATIONAL MEDICAL CORPS

Since its inception in 1984, International Medical Corps' mission has been consistent: relieve the suffering of those impacted by war, natural disaster, and disease by delivering vital health care services that focus on training. This approach of helping people help themselves is critical to returning devastated populations to self-reliance. IMC integrates activities that specifically address the needs of women who are critical to the health and well-being of children, families, communities, and nations. These include mental health, reproductive health, and sexual and gender-based violence awareness, prevention and treatment. In addition, IMC incorporates emergency obstetric care into its programs wherever possible, enabling safe deliveries for high-risk pregnancies. To learn more see www.imcworldwide.org

International Medical Corps
1919 Santa Monica Blvd., Suite 300
Santa Monica, California 90404
USA

OXFAM AMERICA

Oxfam America is an international relief and development organization working to end poverty, hunger, and injustice. Together with individuals and local groups in more than 120 countries, Oxfam saves lives, helps people overcome poverty, and fights for social justice.

Seventy percent of the world's poorest people are women and girls—leaving women and their children vulnerable to disease, displacement, famine, and brutality. Around the world, Oxfam plays a key role in protecting women's rights. In Mozambique, Oxfam won a landmark victory with its passage of a law that secured many rights previously denied to women and girls. In El Salvador, where hundreds of women are murdered every year, Oxfam supports a coalition pushing for laws to protect women from violence. In sub-Saharan Africa, women aged fifteen to twenty-four are more than three times as likely to be HIV positive as young men. Because rape and other violence against women are leading factors in HIV infection, Oxfam is promoting an aggressive human-rights-based strategy to address the legal and social factors that endanger the health of women and girls. To join our efforts or learn more, go to www.oxfamaerica.org.

Oxfam America
226 Causeway Street, 5th Floor
Boston, MA 02114
USA

PLANNED PARENTHOOD FEDERATION OF AMERICA

Planned Parenthood is America's leading sexual and reproductive health care advocate and provider. Founded by Margaret Sanger in 1916 as America's first birth control clinic, Planned Parenthood believes that everyone has the right to choose when or whether to have a child, that every child should be wanted and loved, and that women should be in charge of their destinies. To find out how you can take action to protect reproductive rights, to make a donation, or to find the Planned Parenthood health center nearest you, go to www.plannedparenthood.org.

THE HEIFER PROJECT INTERNATIONAL

Founded in 1944, Heifer International is a humanitarian assistance organization that works to end world hunger and protect the earth. Through livestock, training, and "passing on the gift," Heifer has helped seven million families in more than 125 countries improve their quality of life and move toward greater self-reliance. Heifer helps build strong communities because each project participant agrees to pass on the gift of animal offspring, training, or skills to another family in need. To learn more go to www.heifer.org.

Heifer Project International
PO Box 805
Little Rock, AR 72202
USA

WOMEN FOR WOMEN INTERNATIONAL

Women for Women International helps women in war-torn regions rebuild their lives by providing financial and emotional support, job skills, training, rights awareness, and leadership education and access to business skills, capital, and markets. Through the program, women become confident, independent, and productive as they embrace the importance of their roles in rebuilding their families, their communities, and ultimately, their nations. See www.women-forwomen.org.

Women for Women International
4455 Connecticut Avenue Suite 200
Washington DC 20008
USA

DISCUSSION QUESTIONS

BOOK CLUB DISCUSSION QUESTIONS

In *Joy in the Morning*, we don't learn whether Cassandra's beloved jump rope was replaced or not. How does this affect the story?

What can be learned from little Cassandra's positive attitude? Do you see yourself in her? In what ways?

Cassandra is amazingly resilient. What, in your view, makes resiliency like hers possible in a culture of poverty?

Maria Gabriel finds a way of expressing herself even though she is oppressed. In what other ways do oppressed women find to express themselves? In what ways can women, oppressed or not, support each other?

Discuss your reaction to the writer's statement in the story *Maria Gabriel* that "Women need time with other women. It's a natural cycle." Do you agree with this statement or disagree and why?

Women in every culture are often given the message that they are weak and worthless. Discuss how this message might be delivered to them overtly or covertly. In what ways do the women of *Womankind* demonstrate their strengths and value?

In *Dance Baby Girl Dance*, when Mele's skirt falls during the dance show, there is a split second when the reader does not know whether her mother will help her or not. Tell us what would you have done in the circumstance? Some mothers and daughters have a moment in time suspended in memory when the lesson of separation—that we must each live our own life—becomes clear. Do you have such a moment? Tell us your story.

In *A Picnic in Hoghoost*, Bedrije explains the Albanian-Muslim concept of retribution. Discuss your thoughts upon reading this passage.

Bedreji seems less oppressed than the average woman in Kosovo. What might account for her confidence?

In *The World is a Dangerous Place*, a "landmine" turns out to be simply a large turtle. Have you ever experienced what you thought was a huge problem that turned out to be very small? Tell us your story.

In *The World is a Dangerous Place*, the writer recalls a favorite quote, "Behold the lowly turtle; she only makes progress when she sticks her neck out." What does this mean to you? Do you agree that progress is made by taking risks?

The story *In God's Palm* makes a point about the nutritional plight of women around the world. The American nurse does not buy the formula for baby Em. What are your thoughts regarding this? How would have you reacted in this situation?

In *Over Coffee with Sister Filje*, the nun wears many hats in her village—nurse, social worker, midwife, etc. She might be seen as an example of what women are asked to do in wartime. Discuss the impact of war on women. What are some of the jobs and tasks women are expected to do in times of war they might not be otherwise?

Sister Filje's "miracle" can be seen as just that—a miracle—or it may be explained with a benign medical diagnosis. Which version do you favor? Why?

In *Lillian's Life,* Lillian lives a life of hard work and poverty yet is able to consistently maintain an attitude of gratitude. What do you believe are the sources of her strength? Lillian says, "I have life and life is enough." Discuss this philosophy.

Although outward appearances seemed it impossible, Lillian's life was joy-filled. How do we determine what kind of life is worth living? How would you describe such a life?

In *Please Help My Son Not Die,* the American finds herself in an awkward position of helping the staff adjust to one more change. This speaks to the difficulty most people have of accepting change. Discuss some of the different ways people cope with change.

In *Socorro's Secret,* the teacher treats Nancy like a daughter and advises her cough treatment. We don't know whether it was simply time, antibiotics, or the bougainvillea teat that cured Nancy's cough. Does not knowing add or detract from the story? Have you ever been ill when away from home? Who attended to you? Have you ever tried an alternative health treatment? Tell us your stories.

In *I am a Curandera,* Agripina is left home alone for several days even though she is only eight years old. How did you feel upon reading this? Compare and contrast how children are treated in your culture with hers. Can you understand why it was necessary and perhaps acceptable that Agripina be left behind?

Agripina's story is about listening to our inner wisdom and acting on it. Have you ever had a time when you followed your intuition when making an important decision? Tell us your story.

Agripina's story is also about connection with a Higher Power that guides her life. Some cultures call this God. Where does your strength come from during difficult times?

In *A Rainbow of Gladiolas,* the old woman laying flowers at the feet of statues might be seen as a symbol for something greater that herself. How do you feel about this? Discuss what you believe draws the writer to the tiny chapels and the grand cathedrals of Mexico.

Secrets are hard. In *A Somber Decision,* Delores hides her darkest secret. Can you imagine a circumstance when it might be the right choice to shield those closest to you from the truth? If you chose to, tell us your story.

In *A Somber Decision,* Delores has a difficult childhood after being abandoned by her mother at age nine. In what ways do you feel her life was shaped by her mother's departure to America? Do you view Delores as a survivor or victim? What are her flaws and her strengths?

Delores becomes a symbol for what happens when a women has no access to healthcare, is devalued, and has no one to turn to. There are hundreds of thousands of "Deloreses" everyday worldwide. Discuss your thoughts on this subject.

Norma Jane symbolizes all women who have chosen to stay in an unfaithful relationship. To what extent did Norma Jean let fate dictate her life? To what extent was her life shaped by her choices? Discuss what choices she had, or didn't have. What do you believe kept her in the relationship with her husband forty years ago? What holds her now? It is implied in the story that Norma Jane copes by denial. What other coping mechanisms do women use to survive in difficult circumstances?

In *You Are the Nurse?* the conversation between Therese, Justina, and the nurse stops when grandfather steps outside the hut. What is the meaning of this? As a young women, would you discuss birth control in front of your grandfather? What is the universal message?

The writer intimates that having modern contraception available will change Justina and Terese's lives. Do you agree or disagree with this assumption and why? During your life, what changes have you seen regarding effective methods of contraception? How has this changed, or not changed, women's lives?

In *The Mermaid's Bounty*, Janet lives very simply aboard a sail-boat without the trappings of modern convenience. In what ways is her life similar to a women living in poverty? How is her life different? Do you believe it is possible to live a "fully minimalist" life and be content? Why or why not? Many people begin to simplify their lives as they get older. Perhaps you have begun to do this. Tell us what you have done to make your life simpler. Have these changes made it more meaningful?

In *Only a Nurse*, Marika comes to an important understanding of herself and her work as she realizes the importance of simply "being." How do you feel about this? Discuss the concept of being fully present in the moment—alone or in relationship. Have you had the opportunity simply to be with someone who was experiencing a challenge? Tell us that story.

In *Choices*, the sage orange seller's philosophy, "Life can stretch your soul, or tear your spirit. You choose," resonates with the writer. Discuss this philosophy.

Consistently, the women of *Womankind* seem to have the art of making do with whatever is at hand. Discuss how this is like, or not like, the woman around you.

In some ways, the women in *Womankind* are very different from each other. In many ways they are very much alike. As you were reading the stories, did you admire one or two of the women more than the others? In what ways are these women like the women in your life? In what ways are they different?

$\mathcal{A}$BOUT THE AUTHOR

A self-described "late starter," author Nancy Leigh Harless graduated from Eastern Washington University with a degree in Nursing when she was 37. After working several years as a nurse, largely in the field of Public Health, she returned to school at the University of Texas at Southwest Medical Center to become a Women's Healthcare Nurse Practitioner. Now retired, Nancy divides her time between her home in Wever, Iowa, and traveling around the world—always on a shoestring, usually off the well-traveled road—with her husband, Norm. A blended family, Norm and Nancy share eight children, fourteen grandchildren, and one cat.